# Prefatory Note

This Shakespeare play uses the full Alexander text. By keeping in mind the fact that the language has changed considerably in four hundred years, as have customs, jokes, and stage conventions, the editors have aimed at helping the modern reader – whether English is their mother tongue or not – to grasp the full significance of the play. The Notes, intended primarily for examination candidates, are presented in a simple, direct style. The needs of those unfamiliar with British culture have been specially considered.

Since quiet study of the printed word is unlikely to bring fully to life plays that were written directly for the public theatre, attention has been drawn to dramatic effects which are important in performance. The editors see Shakespeare's plays as living works of art which can be enjoyed today on stage, film and television in many parts of the world.

# THE ALEXANDER SHAKESPEARE

General Edito
R.B. Kennedy

Add
Mike G

# OTHELLO

# William Shakespeare

COLLINS
CLASSICS

Harper Press
An imprint of HarperCollins*Publishers*
77–85 Fulham Palace Road
Hammersmith
London W6 8JB

This Harper Press paperback edition published 2011

A catalogue record for this book is available from the British Library

ISBN-13: 978-0-00-790240-8

Printed and bound in Great Britain by Clays Ltd, St Ives plc

**MIX**
**Paper from
responsible sources**
FSC
www.fsc.org
FSC™ C007454

FSC™ is a non-profit international organisation established to promote
the responsible management of the world's forests. Products carrying the
FSC label are independently certified to assure consumers that they come
from forests that are managed to meet the social, economic and
ecological needs of present and future generations,
and other controlled sources.

Find out more about HarperCollins and the environment at
**www.harpercollins.co.uk/green**

Life & Times section © Gerard Cheshire
Introduction by David Newell
Shakespeare: Words and Phrases adapted from
*Collins English Dictionary*
Typesetting in Kalix by Palimpsest Book Production Limited,
Falkirk, Stirlingshire

10 9 8 7 6 5 4 3 2 1

# CONTENTS

*An Elizabethan playhouse.* Note the apron stage protruding into the auditorium, the space below it, the inner room at the rear of the stage, the gallery above the inner stage, the canopy over the main stage, and the absence of a roof over the audience.

# The Theatre in Shakespeare's Day

On the face of it, the conditions in the Elizabethan theatre were not such as to encourage great writers. The public playhouse itself was not very different from an ordinary inn-yard; it was open to the weather; among the spectators were often louts, pickpockets and prostitutes; some of the actors played up to the rowdy elements in the audience by inserting their own jokes into the authors' lines, while others spoke their words loudly but unfeelingly; the presentation was often rough and noisy, with fireworks to represent storms and battles, and a table and a few chairs to represent a tavern; there were no actresses, so boys took the parts of women, even such subtle and mature ones as Cleopatra and Lady Macbeth; there was rarely any scenery at all in the modern sense. In fact, a quick inspection of the English theatre in the reign of Elizabeth I by a time-traveller from the twentieth century might well produce only one positive reaction: the costumes were often elaborate and beautiful.

Shakespeare himself makes frequent comments in his plays about the limitations of the playhouse and the actors of his time, often apologizing for them. At the beginning of *Henry V* the Prologue refers to the stage as 'this unworthy scaffold' and to the theatre building (the Globe, probably) as 'this wooden O', and emphasizes the urgent need for imagination in making up for all the deficiencies of presentation. In introducing Act IV the Chorus goes so far as to say:

> . . . we shall much disgrace
> With four or five most vile and ragged foils,
> Right ill-dispos'd in brawl ridiculous,
> The name of Agincourt, (lines 49–52)

In *A Midsummer Night's Dream* (Act V, Scene i) he seems to dismiss actors with the words:

The best in this kind are but shadows.

Yet Elizabeth's theatre, with all its faults, stimulated dramatists to a variety of achievement that has never been equalled and, in Shakespeare, produced one of the greatest writers in history. In spite of all his grumbles he seems to have been fascinated by the challenge that it presented him with. It is necessary to re-examine his theatre carefully in order to understand how he was able to achieve so much with the materials he chose to use. What sort of place was the Elizabethan playhouse in reality? What sort of people were these criticized actors? And what sort of audiences gave them their living?

# The Development of the Theatre up to Shakespeare's Time

For centuries in England noblemen had employed groups of skilled people to entertain them when required. Under Tudor rule, as England became more secure and united, actors such as these were given more freedom, and they often performed in public, while still acknowledging their 'overlords' (in the 1570s, for example, when Shakespeare was still a schoolboy at Stratford, one famous company was called 'Lord Leicester's Men'). London was rapidly becoming larger and more important in the second half of the sixteenth century, and many of the companies of actors took the opportunities offered to establish themselves at inns on the main roads leading to the City (for example, the Boar's Head in Whitechapel and the Tabard in South-wark) or in the City itself. These groups of actors would come to an agreement with the inn-keeper which would give them the use of the yard for their performances after people had eaten and drunk well in the middle of the day. Before long, some inns were taken over completely by companies of players and thus became the first public theatres. In 1574 the officials of the City of London issued an order which shows clearly that these theatres were both popular and also offensive to some respectable people, because the order complains about 'the inordinate haunting of great multitudes of people, specially youth, to plays interludes and shows; namely occasion of frays and quarrels, evil practices of incontinency in great inns . . .' There is evidence that, on public holidays, the theatres on the banks of the Thames were crowded with noisy apprentices and tradesmen, but it would be wrong to think that audiences were always undiscriminating and loudmouthed. In spite of the disapproval of Puritans and the more staid members of society, by the 1590s, when Shakespeare's plays were beginning to be performed, audiences consisted of a good cross-section of English society, nobility as well as workers, intellectuals as well as simple people out for a laugh; also (and in this respect English theatres were unique in Europe), it was quite normal for respectable women to attend plays. So Shakespeare had to write plays which would appeal to people of widely different kinds. He had to provide 'something for everyone' but at the same time to take care to unify the material so that it would not seem to fall into separate pieces as they watched it. A speech like that of the drunken porter in *Macbeth* could provide the 'groundlings' with a belly-laugh, but also held a deeper significance for those who could appreciate it. The audience he wrote for was one of a number of apparent drawbacks which Shakespeare was able to turn to his and our advantage.

# Shakespeare's Actors

Nor were all the actors of the time mere 'rogues, vagabonds and sturdy beggars' as some were described in a Statute of 1572. It is true that many of them had a hard life and earned very little money, but leading actors could become partners in the ownership of the theatres in which they acted: Shakespeare was a shareholder in the Globe and the Blackfriars theatres when he was an actor as well as a playwright. In any case, the attacks made on Elizabethan actors were usually directed at their morals and not at their acting ability; it is clear that many of them must have been good at their trade if they were able to interpret complex works like the great tragedies in such a way as to attract enthusiastic audiences. Undoubtedly some of the boys took the women's parts with skill and confidence, since a man called Coryate, visiting Venice in 1611, expressed surprise that women could act as well as they: 'I saw women act, a thing that I never saw before . . . and they performed it with as good a grace, action, gesture . . . as ever I saw any masculine actor.' The quality of most of the actors who first presented Shakespeare's plays is probably accurately summed up by Fynes Moryson, who wrote, '. . . as there be, in my opinion, more plays in London than in all the parts of the world I have seen, so do these players or comedians excel all other in the world.'

# The Structure of the Public Theatre

Although the 'purpose-built' theatres were based on the inn-yards which had been used for play-acting, most of them were circular. The walls contained galleries on three storeys from which the wealthier patrons watched, they must have been something like the 'boxes' in a modern theatre, except that they held much larger numbers – as many as 1500. The 'groundlings' stood on the floor of the building, facing a raised stage which projected from the 'stage-wall', the main features of which were:

1 a small room opening on to the back of the main stage and on the same level as it (rear stage),
2 a gallery above this inner stage (upper stage),
3 canopy projecting from above the gallery over the main stage, to protect the actors from the weather (the 700 or 800 members of the audience who occupied the yard, or 'pit' as we call it today, had the sky above them).

In addition to these features there were dressing-rooms behind the stage and a space underneath it from which entrances could be made through trap-doors. All the acting areas – main stage, rear stage, upper stage and under stage – could be entered by actors directly from their dressing rooms, and all of them were used in productions of Shakespeare's plays. For example, the inner stage, an almost cavelike structure, would have been where Ferdinand and Miranda are 'discovered' playing chess in the last act of *The Tempest*, while the upper stage was certainly the balcony from which Romeo climbs down in Act III of *Romeo and Juliet*.

It can be seen that such a building, simple but adaptable, was not really unsuited to the presentation of plays like Shakespeare's. On the contrary, its simplicity guaranteed the minimum of distraction, while its shape and construction must have produced a sense of involvement on the part of the audience that modern producers would envy.

# Other Resources of the Elizabethan Theatre

Although there were few attempts at scenery in the public theatre (painted backcloths were occasionally used in court performances), Shakespeare and his fellow playwrights were able to make use of a fair variety of 'properties', lists of such articles have survived: they include beds, tables, thrones, and also trees, walls, a gallows, a Trojan horse and a 'Mouth of Hell'; in a list of properties belonging to the manager, Philip Henslowe, the curious item 'two mossy banks' appears. Possibly one of them was used for the

> bank whereon the wild thyme blows,
> Where oxlips and the nodding violet grows

in *A Midsummer Night's Dream* (Act II, Scene i). Once again, imagination must have been required of the audience.

Costumes were the one aspect of stage production in which

trouble and expense were hardly ever spared to obtain a magnificent effect. Only occasionally did they attempt any historical accuracy (almost all Elizabethan productions were what we should call 'modern-dress' ones), but they were appropriate to the characters who wore them: kings were seen to be kings and beggars were similarly unmistakable. It is an odd fact that there was usually no attempt at illusion in the costuming: if a costume looked fine and rich it probably was. Indeed, some of the costumes were almost unbelievably expensive. Henslowe lent his company £19 to buy a cloak, and the Alleyn brothers, well-known actors, gave £20 for a 'black velvet cloak, with sleeves embroidered all with silver and gold, lined with black satin striped with gold'.

With the one exception of the costumes, the 'machinery' of the playhouse was economical and uncomplicated rather than crude and rough, as we can see from this second and more leisurely look at it. This meant that playwrights were stimulated to produce the imaginative effects that they wanted from the language that they used. In the case of a really great writer like Shakespeare, when he had learned his trade in the theatre as an actor, it seems that he received quite enough assistance of a mechanical and structural kind without having irksome restrictions and conventions imposed on him; it is interesting to try to guess what he would have done with the highly complex apparatus of a modern television studio. We can see when we look back to his time that he used his instrument, the Elizabethan theatre, to the full, but placed his ultimate reliance on the communication between his imagination and that of his audience through the medium of words. It is, above all, his rich and wonderful use of language that must have made play-going at that time a memorable experience for people of widely different kinds. Fortunately, the deep satisfaction of appreciating and enjoying Shakespeare's work can be ours also, if we are willing to overcome the language difficulty produced by the passing of time.

# Shakespeare: A Timeline

Very little indeed is known about Shakespeare's private life; the facts included here are almost the only indisputable ones. The dates of Shakespeare's plays are those on which they were first produced.

1558  Queen Elizabeth crowned.

1561  Francis Bacon born.

1564  Christopher Marlowe born.

William Shakespeare born, April 23rd, baptized April 26th.

1566

Shakespeare's brother, Gilbert, born.

1567  Mary, Queen of Scots, deposed.
James VI (later James I of England) crowned King of Scotland.

1572  Ben Jonson born.
Lord Leicester's Company (of players) licensed; later called Lord Strange's, then the Lord Chamberlain's and finally (under James) the King's Men.

1573  John Donne born.

1574  The Common Council of London directs that all plays and playhouses in London must be licensed.

1576  James Burbage builds the first public playhouse, The Theatre, at Shoreditch, outside the walls of the City.

1577  Francis Drake begins his voyage round the world (completed 1580).
*Holinshed's Chronicles of England, Scotland and Ireland* published (which

Shakespeare later used extensively).

| | | |
|---|---|---|
| 1582 | | Shakespeare married to Anne Hathaway. |
| 1583 | The Queen's Company founded by royal warrant. | Shakespeare's daughter, Susanna, born. |
| 1585 | | Shakespeare's twins, Hamnet and Judith, born. |
| 1586 | Sir Philip Sidney, the Elizabethan ideal 'Christian knight', poet, patron, soldier, killed at Zutphen in the Low Countries. | |
| 1587 | Mary, Queen of Scots, beheaded. Marlowe's *Tamburlaine (Part I)* first staged. | |
| 1588 | Defeat of the Spanish Armada. Marlowe's *Tamburlaine (Part II)* first staged. | |
| 1589 | Marlowe's *Jew of Malta* and Kyd's *Spanish Tragedy* (a 'revenge tragedy' and one of the most popular plays of Elizabethan times). | |
| 1590 | Spenser's *Faerie Queene* (Books I–III) published. | |
| 1592 | Marlowe's *Doctor Faustus* and *Edward II* first staged. Witchcraft trials in Scotland. Robert Greene, a rival playwright, refers to Shakespeare as 'an upstart crow' and 'the only Shake-scene in a country'. | *Titus Andronicus* *Henry VI, Parts I, II and III* *Richard III* |
| 1593 | London theatres closed by the plague. Christopher Marlowe killed in a Deptford tavern. | *Two Gentlemen of Verona* *Comedy of Errors* *The Taming of the Shrew* *Love's Labour's Lost* |
| 1594 | Shakespeare's company becomes The Lord Chamberlain's Men. | *Romeo and Juliet* |

| 1595 | Raleigh's first expedition to Guiana. Last expedition of Drake and Hawkins (both died). | *Richard II* <br> *A Midsummer Night's Dream* |
| --- | --- | --- |
| 1596 | Spenser's *Faerie Queene* (Books IV–VI) published. James Burbage buys rooms at Blackfriars and begins to convert them into a theatre. | *King John* <br> *The Merchant of Venice* <br> Shakespeare's son Hamnet dies. <br> Shakespeare's father is granted a coat of arms. |
| 1597 | James Burbage dies, his son Richard, a famous actor, turns the Blackfriars Theatre into a private playhouse. | *Henry IV (Part I)* <br> Shakespeare buys and redecorates New Place at Stratford. |
| 1598 | Death of Philip II of Spain | *Henry IV (Part II)* <br> *Much Ado About Nothing* |
| 1599 | Death of Edmund Spenser. The Globe Theatre completed at Bankside by Richard and Cuthbert Burbage. | *Henry V* <br> *Julius Caesar* <br> *As You Like It* |
| 1600 | Fortune Theatre built at Cripplegate. East India Company founded for the extension of English trade and influence in the East. The Children of the Chapel begin to use the hall at Blackfriars. | *Merry Wives of Windsor* <br> *Troilus and Cressida* |
| 1601 | | *Hamlet* |
| 1602 | Sir Thomas Bodley's library opened at Oxford. | *Twelfth Night* |
| 1603 | Death of Queen Elizabeth. James I comes to the throne. Shakespeare's company becomes The King's Men. Raleigh tried, condemned and sent to the Tower | |
| 1604 | Treaty of peace with Spain | *Measure for Measure* <br> *Othello* <br> *All's Well that Ends Well* |
| 1605 | The Gunpowder Plot: an attempt by a group of Catholics to blow up the Houses of Parliament. | |

| 1606 | Guy Fawkes and other plotters executed. | *Macbeth*<br>*King Lear* |
|---|---|---|
| 1607 | Virginia, in America, colonized.<br>A great frost in England. | *Antony and Cleopatra*<br>*Timon of Athens*<br>*Coriolanus*<br>Shakespeare's daughter, Susanna, married to Dr. John Hall. |
| 1608 | The company of the Children of the Chapel Royal (who had performed at Blackfriars for ten years) is disbanded. John Milton born.<br>Notorious pirates executed in London. | Richard Burbage leases the Blackfriars Theatre to six of his fellow actors, including Shakespeare.<br>*Pericles, Prince of Tyre* |
| 1609 | | Shakespeare's Sonnets published. |
| 1610 | A great drought in England | *Cymbeline* |
| 1611 | Chapman completes his great translation of the *Iliad*, the story of Troy.<br>Authorized Version of the Bible published. | *A Winter's Tale*<br>*The Tempest* |
| 1612 | Webster's *The White Devil* first staged. | Shakespeare's brother, Gilbert, dies. |
| 1613 | Globe theatre burnt down during a performance of *Henry VIII* (the firing of small cannon set fire to the thatched roof).<br>Webster's *Duchess of Malfi* first staged. | *Henry VIII*<br>*Two Noble Kinsmen*<br>Shakespeare buys a house at Blackfriars. |
| 1614 | Globe Theatre rebuilt in 'far finer manner than before'. | |
| 1616 | Ben Jonson publishes his plays in one volume.<br>Raleigh released from the Tower in order to prepare an expedition to the gold mines of Guiana. | Shakespeare's daughter, Judith, marries Thomas Quiney.<br>Death of Shakespeare on his birthday, April 23rd. |
| 1618 | Raleigh returns to England and is executed on the charge for which he was imprisoned in 1603. | |
| 1623 | Publication of the Folio edition of Shakespeare's plays | Death of Anne Shakespeare (née Hathaway). |

# Life & Times

## William Shakespeare the Playwright

There exists a curious paradox when it comes to the life of William Shakespeare. He easily has more words written about him than any other famous English writer, yet we know the least about him. This inevitably means that most of what is written about him is either fabrication or speculation. The reason why so little is known about Shakespeare is that he wasn't a novelist or a historian or a man of letters. He was a playwright, and playwrights were considered fairly low on the social pecking order in Elizabethan society. Writing plays was about providing entertainment for the masses – the great unwashed. It was the equivalent to being a journalist for a tabloid newspaper.

In fact, we only know of Shakespeare's work because two of his friends had the foresight to collect his plays together following his death and have them printed. The only reason they did so was apparently because they rated his talent and thought it would be a shame if his words were lost.

Consequently his body of work has ever since been assessed and reassessed as the greatest contribution to English literature. That is despite the fact that we know that different printers took it upon themselves to heavily edit the material they worked from. We also know that Elizabethan plays were worked and reworked frequently, so that they evolved over time until they were honed to perfection, which means that many different hands played their part in the active writing process. It would therefore be fair to say that any play attributed to Shakespeare is unlikely to contain a great deal of original input. Even the plots were based on well known historical events, so it would be hard to know what fragments of any Shakespeare play came from that single mind.

One might draw a comparison with the Christian bible, which remains such a compelling read because it came from the collaboration of many contributors and translators over centuries, who each adjusted the stories until they could no longer be improved. As virtually nothing is known of Shakespeare's life and even less about his method of working, we shall never know the truth about his plays. They certainly contain some very elegant phrasing, clever plot devices and plenty of words never before seen in print, but as to whether Shakespeare invented them from a unique imagination or whether he simply took them from others around him is anyone's guess.

The best bet seems to be that Shakespeare probably took the lead role in devising the original drafts of the plays, but was open to collaboration from any source when it came to developing them into workable scripts for effective performances. He would have had to work closely with his fellow actors in rehearsals, thereby finding out where to edit, abridge, alter, reword and so on.

In turn, similar adjustments would have occurred in his absence, so that definitive versions of his plays never really existed. In effect Shakespeare was only responsible for providing the framework of plays, upon which others took liberties over time. This wasn't helped by the fact that the English language itself was not definitive at that time either. The consequence was that people took it upon themselves to spell words however they pleased or to completely change words and phrasing to suit their own preferences.

It is easy to see then, that Shakespeare's plays were always going to have lives of their own, mutating and distorting in detail like Chinese whispers. The culture of creative preservation was simply not established in Elizabethan England. Creative ownership of Shakespeare's plays was lost to him as soon as he released them into the consciousness of others. They saw nothing wrong with taking his ideas and running with them, because no one had ever suggested that one shouldn't, and Shakespeare probably regarded his work in the same way. His plays weren't sacrosanct works of art, they were templates for theatre folk to make their livings from, so they had every right to mould them into productions that drew in the crowds as effectively as possible. Shakespeare was like the helmsman of a sailing ship, steering the vessel but wholly reliant on the team work of his crew to arrive at the desired destination.

It seems that Shakespeare certainly had a natural gift, but the genius of his plays may be attributable to the collective efforts of Shakespeare and others. It is a rather satisfying notion to think that *his* plays might actually be the creative outpourings of the Elizabethan milieu in which Shakespeare immersed himself. That makes them important social documents as well as seminal works of the English language.

# Money in Shakespeare's Day

It is extremely difficult, if not impossible, to relate the value of money in our time to its value in another age and to compare prices of commodities today and in the past. Many items *are* simply not comparable on grounds of quality or serviceability.

There was a bewildering variety of coins in use in Elizabethan England. As nearly all English and European coins were gold or silver, they had intrinsic value apart from their official value. This meant that foreign coins circulated freely in England and were officially recognized, for example the French crown (écu) worth about 30p (72 cents), and the Spanish ducat worth about 33p (79 cents). The following table shows some of the coins mentioned by Shakespeare and their relation to one another.

| GOLD | British | American | SILVER | British | American |
|---|---|---|---|---|---|
| sovereign (heavy type) | £1.50 | $3.60 | shilling | 10p | 24c |
| sovereign (light type) | 66p–£1 | $1.58–$2.40 | groat | 1.5p | 4c |
| angel royal | 33p–50p | 79c–$1.20 | | | |
| noble | 50p | $1.20 | | | |
| crown | 25p | 60c | | | |

A comparison of the following prices in Shakespeare's time with the prices of the same items today will give some idea of the change in the value of money.

| ITEM | PRICE British | American | ITEM | PRICE British | American |
|---|---|---|---|---|---|
| beef, per lb. | 0.5p | 1c | cherries (lb.) | 1p | 2c |
| mutton, leg | 7.5p | 18c | 7 oranges | 1p | 2c |
| rabbit | 3.5p | 9c | 1 lemon | 1p | 2c |
| chicken | 3p | 8c | cream (quart) | 2.5p | 6c |
| potatoes (lb) | 10p | 24c | sugar (lb.) | £1 | $2.40 |
| carrots (bunch) | 1p | 2c | sack (wine) (gallon) | 14p | 34c |
| 8 artichokes | 4p | 9c | tobacco (oz.) | 25p | 60c |
| 1 cucumber | 1p | 2c | biscuits (lb.) | 12.5p | 30c |

# INTRODUCTION

*Othello* is a play about a black man in a white man's world. A public servant with a private life, an older man who marries a mere girl, a soldier who exchanges the battlefield for the bedroom: incongruity is pervasive. So too is incomprehension, for if Othello is an unknown quantity because of his mysterious background, Venetian customs are equally outside his experience. Mutual misunderstanding underlies the chaos of this exquisitely painful domestic tragedy.

Our initial perception of Othello is masterminded, as is so much in this drama, by Iago. His opening conversation with Roderigo and his ribald taunting of Brabantio sketch for us a barbaric, incontinent savage, a typical stage negro. But that image is shattered the very first time the audience encounters the Moor. In his calm dignity, courage, and urbane courtesy he seems to step straight off the pages of Castiglione's *Courtier*. Beside him the native Venetians appear trivial, dwarfed by his presence and silenced by his poetry. Othello's life is rooted deep in his language; that is the outward expression of his inner being, a dramatic symbol of the imaginative richness which he represents. Further, he is efficient as a military commander and well respected by the state.

Othello starts the play, then, as an epic warrior hero of classical grandeur, a man of strange experiences, foreign parts, and a distinctive vocal timbre. But the crafty and malicious manipulation of Iago transforms him into the contemptible butt of traditional domestic comedy – the jealous, cuckolded husband. Yet it is not Iago's skill alone which effects this metamorphosis. The entire play seems to undergo a generic shift. It starts at the point where romantic comedy normally ends, with a happy, if unusual, marriage and the marginalising of an irate father. But

then a hasty switch of setting to Cyprus, far from repli-
cating the security of a fantasy world like Belmont or the
holiday fun of Arden, steers the play into turmoil. Away
from Italian civilisation but curiously closer to the forbid-
ding continent of Othello's birth, the lovers are perversely
abandoned by Fortune. Events consistently work against
them. Cassio is sighted slipping suspiciously away from
Othello's house; the handkerchief happens to be dropped
and found just when Iago needs tangible proof; Cassio
and Bianca converse out of Othello's earshot so that he
can misconstrue their meaning. Characters disconcert-
ingly change. Desdemona loses the poise and self-possession
which marked her defence before the Venetian Senate,
and dwindles into a child-wife, naive, frustratingly inept,
and vulnerable.

Most significant of all, Othello himself compromises
the heroism of epic warfare with the visual physical frenzy
of tawdry comedy: eavesdropping, falling to the ground,
beating his wife. Worse, he seems at these moments to
be the helpless puppet of Iago. As his actions are cheap-
ened, so too is his speech. Iago was the first to deconstruct
Othello's language ('a bombast circumstance/Horribly
stuff'd with epithets of war'), and he has not been the
last. But then Iago cannot stomach poetry. And what he
cannot enjoy he must destroy. But not even Iago can
erase the audience's memory, for words once spoken
linger, enshrined in a text. At his worst moments we are
never allowed to forget what Othello was:

> Is this the noble Moor whom our full Senate
> Call all in all sufficient? Is this the nature
> Whom passion could not shake, whose solid virtue
> The shot of accident nor dart of chance
> Could neither graze nor pierce?          [4.1.261–5]

Iago's plan to humiliate Othello is ultimately and ironi-
cally hijacked by the play itself, which takes on a
momentum of its own, bringing Othello through the

degradation of comic gull to the new status of tragic hero. The revival of Othello's speech in his last visit to Desdemona's bedchamber, the dawning recognition of his error, and the reenactment of a past deed of justice in his suicide all combine to make him much more than Iago's dupe. At the very end it is Iago who remains sullenly silent, finally upstaged by Othello, who is allowed the privilege of speaking his own epitaph and passing judgement on his own crime.

The deaths of Brabantio's runaway daughter and the mercenary black soldier create no cosmic ripples. There are no emblematic storms, no upheavals in the body politic. The world outside goes on much as usual. This, far from diminishing, only intensifies the tragedy of two innocents in an unsympathetic, deceiving world. And when misunderstandings are finally over as white girl and black man are reunited in the stage tableau of death, we may find that the only adequate response was uttered long ago:

O, Iago, the pity of it, Iago! [4.1.191]

# LIST OF CHARACTERS

| | |
|---|---|
| *Duke Of Venice* | a Senator, father to Desdemona |
| *Brabantio* | |
| *Other Senators* | |
| *Gratiano* | brother to Brabantio, two noble Venetians |
| *Lodovico* | kinsman to Brabantio |
| *Othello* | the Moor, in the service of Venice |
| *Cassio* | his honourable Lieutenant |
| *Iago* | his Ancient, a villain |
| *Roderigo* | a gull'd Venetian gentleman |
| *Montano* | Governor of Cyprus, before Othello |
| *Clown servant to Othello* | |
| *Desdemona* | daughter to Brabantio, and wife to Othello |
| *Emilia* | wife to Iago |
| *Bianca* | a courtezan, in love with Cassio |

*Gentlemen of Cyprus, Sailors, Officers, a Messenger, Musicians, a Herald, and Attendants etc.*

**The Scene:** Venice; Cyprus.

# ACT ONE
## SCENE I

### Venice. A street.

*[Enter* RODERIGO *and* IAGO.*]*

**Roderigo**
　　Tush, never tell me; I take it much unkindly
　　That you, Iago, who has had my purse
　　As if the strings were thine, shouldst know of this.
**Iago**
　　'Sblood, but you will not hear me.
　　If ever I did dream of such a matter,　　　　　　5
　　Abhor me.
**Roderigo**
　　Thou told'st me thou didst hold him in thy hate.
**Iago**
　　Despise me if I do not. Three great ones of the city,
　　In personal suit to make me his lieutenant,
　　Off-capp'd to him; and, by the faith of man,　　10
　　I know my price, I am worth no worse a place.
　　But he, as loving his own pride and purposes,
　　Evades them with a bombast circumstance
　　Horribly stuff'd with epithets of war;
　　And, in conclusion,　　　　　　　　　　　　15
　　Nonsuits my mediators; 'For, certes,' says he
　　'I have already chose my officer'.
　　And what was he?
　　Forsooth, a great arithmetician,
　　One Michael Cassio, a Florentine,　　　　　　20
　　A fellow almost damn'd in a fair wife,
　　That never set a squadron in the field,
　　Nor the division of a battle knows
　　More than a spinster; unless the bookish theoric,
　　Wherein the toged consuls can propose　　　　25

As masterly as he – mere prattle, without practice,
Is all his soldiership. But he, sir, had the election;
And I, of whom his eyes had seen the proof
At Rhodes, at Cyprus, and on other grounds,
30    Christian and heathen, must be be-lee'd and calm'd
By debitor and creditor – this counter-caster,
He, in good time, must his lieutenant be,
And I, God bless the mark! his Moorship's ancient.

*Roderigo*

By heaven, I rather would have been his hangman!

*Iago*

35    Why, there's no remedy; 'tis the curse of service:
Preferment goes by letter and affection,
Not by the old gradation, where each second
Stood heir to the first. Now, sir, be judge yourself
Whether I in any just term am affin'd
To love the Moor.

*Roderigo*

40                     I would not follow him, then.

*Iago*

O, sir, content you.
I follow him to serve my turn upon him:
We cannot all be masters, nor all masters
Cannot be truly follow'd. You shall mark
45    Many a duteous and knee-crooking knave
That, doting on his own obsequious bondage,
Wears out his time, much like his master's ass,
For nought but provender; and when he's old,
    cashier'd.
Whip me such honest knaves. Others there are
50    Who, trimm'd in forms and visages of duty,
Keep yet their hearts attending on themselves;
And, throwing but shows of service on their lords,
Do well thrive by 'em and, when they have lin'd
    their coats,
Do themselves homage – these fellows have some
    soul;

And such a one do I profess myself.                    55
For, sir,
It is as sure as you are Roderigo,
Were I the Moor, I would not be Iago.
In following him I follow but myself –
Heaven is my judge, not I for love and duty,          60
But seeming so for my peculiar end.
For when my outward action doth demonstrate
The native act and figure of my heart
In compliment extern, 'tis not long after
But I will wear my heart upon my sleeve              65
For daws to peck at: I am not what I am.

Roderigo
What a full fortune does the thick-lips owe,
If he can carry't thus!

Iago
                              Call up her father.
Rouse him, make after him, poison his delight,
Proclaim him in the streets; incense her kinsmen,    70
And, though he in a fertile climate dwell,
Plague him with flies; though that his joy be joy,
Yet throw such changes of vexation on't
As it may lose some colour.

Roderigo
Here is her father's house. I'll call aloud.          75

Iago
Do, with like timorous accent and dire yell
As when, by night and negligence, the fire
Is spied in populous cities.

Roderigo
What, ho, Brabantio! Signior Brabantio, ho!

Iago
Awake! What, ho, Brabantio! Thieves, thieves,        80
    thieves!
Look to your house, your daughter, and your bags.
Thieves! thieves!

[BRABANTIO *appears above at a window.*]

*Brabantio*

    What is the reason of this terrible summons?

    What is the matter there?

*Roderigo*

85   Signior, is all your family within?

*Iago*

    Are your doors lock'd?

*Brabantio*

                    Why, wherefore ask you this?

*Iago*

    Zounds, sir, you're robb'd; for shame, put on your
        gown;

    Your heart is burst; you have lost half your soul.

    Even now, now, very now, an old black ram

90   Is tupping your white ewe. Arise, arise;

    Awake the snorting citizens with the bell,

    Or else the devil will make a grandsire of you.

    Arise, I say.

*Brabantio*

             What, have you lost your wits?

*Roderigo*

    Most reverend signior, do you know my voice?

*Brabantio*

95   Not I; what are you?

*Roderigo*

    My name is Roderigo.

*Brabantio*

                   The worser welcome!

    I have charg'd thee not to haunt about my doors;

    In honest plainness thou hast heard me say

    My daughter is not for thee; and now, in madness,

100  Being full of supper and distempering draughts,

    Upon malicious bravery dost thou come

    To start my quiet.

*Roderigo*

    Sir, sir, sir –

*Brabantio*
>>>But thou must needs be sure
My spirit and my place have in their power
To make this bitter to thee.

*Roderigo*
>>>>>>>Patience, good sir.    105

*Brabantio*
What tell'st thou me of robbing? This is Venice;
My house is not a grange.

*Roderigo*
>>>>>>Most grave Brabantio,
In simple and pure soul I come to you.

*Iago*
Zounds, sir, you are one of those that will not serve
God if the devil bid you. Because we come to do you 110
service, and you think we are ruffians, you'll have your
daughter cover'd with a Barbary horse; you'll have your
nephews neigh to you; you'll have coursers for cousins
and gennets for germans.

*Brabantio*
What profane wretch art thou?    115

*Iago*
I am one, sir, that comes to tell you your daughter
and the Moor are now making the beast with two
backs.

*Brabantio*
Thou art a villain.

*Iago*
>>>>>You are – a Senator.

*Brabantio*
This thou shalt answer; I know thee, Roderigo.    120

*Roderigo*
Sir, I will answer anything. But I beseech you,
If't be your pleasure and most wise consent –
As partly I find it is – that your fair daughter,
At this odd-even and dull watch o' th' night,
Transported with no worse nor better guard    125

But with a knave of common hire, a gondolier,
To the gross clasps of a lascivious Moor –
If this be known to you, and your allowance,
We then have done you bold and saucy wrongs;
130 But if you know not this, my manners tell me
We have your wrong rebuke. Do not believe
That, from the sense of all civility,
I thus would play and trifle with your reverence.
Your daughter, if you have not given her leave,
135 I say again, hath made a gross revolt;
Tying her duty, beauty, wit, and fortunes,
In an extravagant and wheeling stranger
Of here and everywhere. Straight satisfy yourself.
If she be in her chamber or your house,
140 Let loose on me the justice of the state
For thus deluding you.

**Brabantio**
Strike on the tinder, ho! Give me a taper; call up all
my people.
This accident is not unlike my dream.
Belief of it oppresses me already.
Light, I say; light!

*[Exit from above.]*

**Iago**
145                    Farewell; for I must leave you.
It seems not meet nor wholesome to my place
To be producted – as if I stay I shall –
Against the Moor; for I do know the state,
However this may gall him with some check,
150 Cannot with safety cast him; for he's embark'd
With such loud reason to the Cyprus wars,
Which even now stands in act, that, for their souls,
Another of his fathom they have none
To lead their business; in which regard,
155 Though I do hate him as I do hell pains,
Yet, for necessity of present life,

I must show out a flag and sign of love,
Which is indeed but sign. That you shall surely find
   him,
Lead to the Sagittary the raised search;
And there will I be with him. So, farewell.       160

*[Exit.]*

*[Enter below,* BRABANTIO, *in his night gown, and
Servants with torches.]*

*Brabantio*
   It is too true an evil. Gone she is;
   And what's to come of my despised time
   Is nought but bitterness. Now, Roderigo,
   Where didst thou see her? – O unhappy girl! –
   With the Moor, say'st thou? – Who would be a
      father? –       165
   How didst thou know 'twas she? – O, thou deceivest
      me
   Past thought! – What said she to you? – Get moe
      tapers;
   Raise all my kindred. – Are they married think you?
*Roderigo*
   Truly, I think they are.
*Brabantio*
   O heaven! How got she out? O treason of the blood! 170
   Fathers, from hence trust not your daughters' minds
   By what you see them act. Is there not charms
   By which the property of youth and maidhood
   May be abus'd? Have you not read, Roderigo,
   Of some such thing?
*Roderigo*
               Yes, sir, I have indeed.      175
*Brabantio*
   Call up my brother. – O that you had had her! –
   Some one way, some another. – Do you know
   Where we may apprehend her and the Moor?

*Roderigo*
  I think I can discover him, if you please
180  To get good guard, and go along with me.
*Brabantio*
  Pray lead me on. At every house I'll call;
  I may command at most. – Get weapons, ho!
  And raise some special officers of night. –
  On, good Roderigo; I'll deserve your pains.

*[Exeunt]*

# SCENE II

### Venice. Another street.

*[Enter* OTHELLO, IAGO, *and Attendants with torches.]*

*Iago*
    Though in the trade of war I have slain men,
    Yet do I hold it very stuff o' th' conscience
    To do no contriv'd murder. I lack iniquity
    Sometime to do me service. Nine or ten times
    I had thought to have yerk'd him here under the ribs.    5

*Othello*
    'Tis better as it is.

*Iago*
            Nay, but he prated,
    And spoke such scurvy and provoking terms
    Against your honour
    That, with the little godliness I have,
    I did full hard forbear him. But I pray, sir,    10
    Are you fast married? For be assur'd of this,
    That the magnifico is much beloved,
    And hath in his effect a voice potential
    As double as the Duke's. He will divorce you,
    Or put upon you what restraint and grievance    15
    That law, with all his might to enforce it on,
    Will give him cable.

*Othello*
            Let him do his spite.
    My services which I have done the signiory
    Shall out-tongue his complaints. 'Tis yet to know –
    Which, when I know that boasting is an honour,    20
    I shall promulgate – I fetch my life and being
    From men of royal siege; and my demerits
    May speak unbonneted to as proud a fortune
    As this that I have reach'd. For know, Iago,
    But that I love the gentle Desdemona,    25
    I would not my unhoused free condition

Put into circumscription and confine
For the seas' worth.

*[Enter* CASSIO *and Officers with torches.]*

But look what lights come yonder.

*Iago*

Those are the raised father and his friends.
You were best go in.

*Othello*

30                        Not I; I must be found.
My parts, my title, and my perfect soul
Shall manifest me rightly. Is it they?

*Iago*

By Janus, I think no.

*Othello*

The servants of the Duke and my lieutenant –
35  The goodness of the night upon you, friends!
What is the news?

*Cassio*

The Duke does greet you, General;
And he requires your haste-post-haste appearance
Even on the instant.

*Othello*

What is the matter, think you?

*Cassio*

40  Something from Cyprus, as I may divine.
It is a business of some heat: the galleys
Have sent a dozen sequent messengers
This very night at one another's heels;
And many of the consuls, rais'd and met,
Are at the Duke's already. You have been hotly call'd
45    for;
When, being not at your lodging to be found,
The Senate hath sent about three several quests
To search you out.

*Othello*

'Tis well I am found by you.

I will but spend a word here in the house,
And go with you. *[Exit.]*

**Cassio**

Ancient, what makes he here?          50

**Iago**

Faith, he to-night hath boarded a land carrack.
If it prove lawful prize, he's made for ever.

**Cassio**

I do not understand.

**Iago**

He's married.

**Cassio**

To who?

*[Re-enter OTHELLO.]*

**Iago**

Marry, to – Come, Captain, will you go?

**Othello**

Have with you.

*[Enter BRABANTIO, RODERIGO, and Officers with torches
and weapons.]*

**Cassio**

Here comes another troop to seek for you.          55

**Iago**

It is Brabantio. General, be advis'd;
He comes to bad intent.

**Othello**

Holla! stand there.

**Roderigo**

Signior, it is the Moor.

**Brabantio**

Down with him, thief.

*[They draw on both sides.]*

**Iago**

You, Roderigo; come, sir, I am for you.

*Othello*

Keep up your bright swords, for the dew will rust
60      them.
Good signior, you shall more command with years
Than with your weapons.

*Brabantio*

O thou foul thief, where hast thou stow'd my
     daughter?
Damn'd as thou art, thou hast enchanted her;
65    For I'll refer me to all things of sense,
If she in chains of magic were not bound,
Whether a maid so tender, fair, and happy,
So opposite to marriage that she shunn'd
The wealthy curled darlings of our nation,
70    Would ever have, to incur a general mock,
Run from her guardage to the sooty bosom
Of such a thing as thou – to fear, not to delight.
Judge me the world, if 'tis not gross in sense
That thou hast practis'd on her with foul charms,
75    Abus'd her delicate youth with drugs or minerals
That weakens motion. I'll have't disputed on;
'Tis probable, and palpable to thinking.
I therefore apprehend and do attach thee
For an abuser of the world, a practiser
80    Of arts inhibited and out of warrant.
Lay hold upon him. If he do resist,
Subdue him at his peril.

*Othello*

                 Hold your hands,
Both you of my inclining and the rest.
Were it my cue to fight, I should have known it
85    Without a prompter. Where will you that I go
To answer this your charge?

*Brabantio*

                     To prison; till fit time
Of law and course of direct session
Call thee to answer.

*Othello*
> What if I do obey?
> How may the Duke be therewith satisfied,
> Whose messengers are here about my side,      90
> Upon some present business of the state,
> To bring me to him.

*Officer*
> 'Tis true, most worthy signior;
> The Duke's in council, and your noble self,
> I am sure, is sent for.

*Brabantio*
> How! The Duke in council!
> In this time of the night! Bring him away.      95
> Mine's not an idle cause. The Duke himself,
> Or any of my brothers of the state,
> Cannot but feel this wrong as 'twere their own;
> For if such actions may have passage free,
> Bond-slaves and pagans shall our statesmen be.      100

*[Exeunt.]*

# SCENE III.

*Venice. A council-chamber.*

*[Enter DUKE and Senators, set at a table with lights; and Attendants.]*

**Duke**
There is no composition in these news
That gives them credit.

**1 Senator**
                    Indeed, they are disproportion'd;
My letters say a hundred and seven galleys.

**Duke**
And mine a hundred and forty.

**2 Senator**
                    And mine two hundred.
5   But though they jump not on a just account –
As in these cases, where the aim reports,
'Tis oft with difference – yet do they all confirm
A Turkish fleet, and bearing up to Cyprus.

**Duke**
Nay, it is possible enough to judgment.
10   I do not so secure me in the error
But the main article I do approve
In fearful sense.

**Sailor**
    *[Within]*        What, ho! what, ho! what, ho!

*[Enter Sailor.]*

**Officer**
A messenger from the galleys.

**Duke**
                    Now, what's the business?

**Sailor**
The Turkish preparation makes for Rhodes;
15   So was I bid report here to the state
By Signior Angelo.

*Duke*
    How say you by this change?
*1 Senator*
                       This cannot be,
    By no assay of reason. 'Tis a pageant
    To keep us in false gaze. When we consider
    The importancy of Cyprus to the Turk,          20
    And let ourselves again but understand
    That as it more concerns the Turk than Rhodes,
    So may he with more facile question bear it,
    For that it stands not in such warlike brace,
    But altogether lacks th' abilities            25
    That Rhodes is dress'd in – if we make thought of
        this,
    We must not think the Turk is so unskilful
    To leave that latest which concerns him first,
    Neglecting an attempt of ease and gain
    To wake and wage a danger profitless.        30
*Duke*
    Nay, in all confidence, he's not for Rhodes.
*Officer*
    Here is more news.

          *[Enter a Messenger.]*

*Messenger*
    The Ottomites, reverend and gracious,
    Steering with due course toward the isle of Rhodes,
    Have there injointed them with an after fleet.    35
*1 Senator*
    Ay, so I thought. How many, as you guess?
*Messenger*
    Of thirty sail; and now they do restem
    Their backward course, bearing with frank
        appearance
    Their purposes toward Cyprus. Signior Montano,
    Your trusty and most valiant servitor,        40
    With his free duty recommends you thus,

And prays you to believe him.

*Duke*

'Tis certain, then, for Cyprus.

Marcus Lucchese, is not he in town?

*1 Senator*

45    He's now in Florence.

*Duke*

Write from us: wish him post-post-haste dispatch.

*[Enter* BRABANTIO, OTHELLO, IAGO, RODERIGO, *and Officers.]*

*1 Senator*

Here comes Brabantio and the valiant Moor.

*Duke*

Valiant Othello, we must straight employ you

Against the general enemy Ottoman.

*[To* BRABANTIO*]* I did not see you; welcome, gentle

50    signior;

We lack'd your counsel and your help to-night.

*Brabantio*

So did I yours. Good your Grace, pardon me:

Neither my place, nor aught I heard of business,

Hath rais'd me from my bed; nor doth the general care

55    Take hold on me; for my particular grief

Is of so flood-gate and o'erbearing nature

That it engluts and swallows other sorrows,

And it is still itself.

*Duke*

Why, what's the matter?

*Brabantio*

My daughter! O, my daughter!

*All*

Dead?

*Brabantio*

Ay, to me.

60    She is abus'd, stol'n from me, and corrupted,

By spells and medicines bought of mountebanks;
For nature so preposterously to err,
Being not deficient, blind, or lame of sense,
Sans witchcraft could not.

**Duke**

Whoe'er he be that in this foul proceeding                    65
Hath thus beguil'd your daughter of herself,
And you of her, the bloody book of law
You shall yourself read in the bitter letter
After your own sense; yea, though our proper son
Stood in your action.

**Brabantio**

              Humbly I thank your Grace.          70
Here is the man – this Moor whom now, it seems,
Your special mandate for the state affairs
Hath hither brought.

**All**

             We are very sorry for't.

**Duke**

[To OTHELLO] What, in your own part, can you say
    to this?

**Brabantio**

Nothing, but this is so.                                     75

**Othello**

Most potent, grave, and reverend signiors,
My very noble and approv'd good masters:
That I have ta'en away this old man's daughter,
It is most true; true, I have married her –
The very head and front of my offending                      80
Hath this extent, no more. Rude am I in my speech,
And little blest with the soft phrase of peace;
For since these arms of mine had seven years' pith,
Till now some nine moons wasted, they have us'd
Their dearest action in the tented field;                    85
And little of this great world can I speak
More than pertains to feats of broil and battle;
And therefore little shall I grace my cause

In speaking for myself. Yet, by your gracious
    patience,
90    I will a round unvarnish'd tale deliver
Of my whole course of love – what drugs, what
    charms,
What conjuration, and what mighty magic,
For such proceedings am I charg'd withal,
I won his daughter.

*Brabantio*

                A maiden never bold,
95    Of spirit so still and quiet that her motion
Blush'd at herself; and she – in spite of nature,
Of years, of country, credit, every thing –
To fall in love with what she fear'd to look on!
It is a judgment maim'd and most imperfect
100   That will confess perfection so could err
Against all rules of nature, and must be driven
To find out practices of cunning hell,
Why this should be. I therefore vouch again
That with some mixtures powerful o'er the blood,
105   Or with some dram conjur'd to this effect,
He wrought upon her.

*Duke*

              To vouch this is no proof –
Without more wider and more overt test
Than these thin habits and poor likelihoods
Of modern seeming do prefer against him.

*1 Senator*

110   But, Othello, speak.
Did you by indirect and forced courses
Subdue and poison this young maid's affections?
Or came it by request, and such fair question
As soul to soul affordeth?

*Othello*

                I do beseech you,
115   Send for the lady to the Sagittary,
And let her speak of me before her father.

If you do find me foul in her report,
The trust, the office, I do hold of you
Not only take away, but let your sentence
Even fall upon my life.

**Duke**

                         Fetch Desdemona hither.      120

**Othello**

Ancient, conduct them; you best know the place.
   *[Exeunt* IAGO *and* ATTENDANTS.*]*
And, till she come, as faithful as to heaven
I do confess the vices of my blood,
So justly to your grave ears I'll present
How I did thrive in this fair lady's love,      125
And she in mine.

**Duke**

Say it, Othello.

**Othello**

Her father lov'd me, oft invited me;
Still question'd me the story of my life
From year to year – the battles, sieges, fortunes,      130
That I have pass'd.
I ran it through, even from my boyish days
To th' very moment that he bade me tell it;
Wherein I spake of most disastrous chances,
Of moving accidents by flood and field;      135
Of hairbreadth scapes i' th' imminent deadly breach;
Of being taken by the insolent foe
And sold to slavery; of my redemption thence,
And portance in my travel's history;
Wherein of antres vast and deserts idle,      140
Rough quarries, rocks, and hills whose heads touch
   heaven,
It was my hint to speak – such was the process;
And of the Cannibals that each other eat,
The Anthropophagi, and men whose heads
Do grow beneath their shoulders. This to hear      145
Would Desdemona seriously incline;

But still the house affairs would draw her thence;
Which ever as she could with haste dispatch,
She'd come again, and with a greedy ear
150 Devour up my discourse. Which I observing,
Took once a pliant hour, and found good means
To draw from her a prayer of earnest heart
That I would all my pilgrimage dilate,
Whereof by parcels she had something heard,
155 But not intentively. I did consent,
And often did beguile her of her tears,
When I did speak of some distressful stroke
That my youth suffer'd. My story being done,
She gave me for my pains a world of sighs;
She swore, in faith, 'twas strange, 'twas passing
160    strange;
'Twas pitiful, 'twas wondrous pitiful.
She wish'd she had not heard it; yet she wish'd
That heaven had made her such a man. She thank'd
   me;
And bade me, if I had a friend that lov'd her,
165 I should but teach him how to tell my story,
And that would woo her. Upon this hint I spake;
She lov'd me for the dangers I had pass'd;
And I lov'd her that she did pity them.
This only is the witchcraft I have us'd.
170 Here comes the lady; let her witness it.

*[Enter DESDEMONA, IAGO, and Attendants.]*

*Duke*
I think this tale would win my daughter too.
Good Brabantio,
Take up this mangled matter at the best.
Men do their broken weapons rather use
Than their bare hands.
*Brabantio*
175               I pray you hear her speak.
If she confess that she was half the wooer,

Destruction on my head if my bad blame
Light on the man! Come hither, gentle mistress.
Do you perceive in all this noble company
Where most you owe obedience?

*Desdemona*

My noble father,     180
I do perceive here a divided duty:
To you I am bound for life and education;
My life and education both do learn me
How to respect you; you are the lord of duty –
I am hitherto your daughter; but here's my husband, 185
And so much duty as my mother show'd
To you, preferring you before her father,
So much I challenge that I may profess
Due to the Moor, my lord.

*Brabantio*

God bu'y, I ha done.
Please it your Grace, on to the state affairs –     190
I had rather to adopt a child than get it.
Come hither, Moor:
I here do give thee that with all my heart
Which, but thou hast already, with all my heart
I would keep from thee. For your sake, jewel,     195
I am glad at soul I have no other child;
For thy escape would teach me tyranny,
To hang clogs on them. I have done, my lord.

*Duke*

Let me speak like yourself, and lay a sentence
Which, as a grise or step, may help these lovers     200
Into your favour.
When remedies are past, the griefs are ended
By seeing the worst, which late on hopes depended.
To mourn a mischief that is past and gone
Is the next way to draw new mischief on.     205
What cannot be preserv'd when fortune takes,
Patience her injury a mockery makes.
The robb'd that smiles steals something from the
     thief;

He robs himself that spends a bootless grief.
*Brabantio*
210 So let the Turk of Cyprus us beguile:
We lose it not so long as we can smile.
He bears the sentence well that nothing bears
But the free comfort which from thence he hears;
But he bears both the sentence and the sorrow
215 That to pay grief must of poor patience borrow.
These sentences, to sugar or to gall,
Being strong on both sides, are equivocal.
But words are words: I never yet did hear
That the bruis'd heart was pierced through the ear.
220 I humbly beseech you proceed to th' affairs of state.
*Duke*
The Turk with a most mighty preparation makes for
Cyprus. Othello, the fortitude of the place is best
known to you; and though we have there a substitute
of most allowed sufficiency, yet opinion, a sovereign
225 mistress of effects, throws a more safer voice on you.
You must therefore be content to slubber the gloss of
your new fortunes with this more stubborn and bois-
terous expedition.
*Othello*
The tyrant custom, most grave senators,
230 Hath made the flinty and steel couch of war
My thrice-driven bed of down. I do agnize
A natural and prompt alacrity
I find in hardness; and would undertake
This present wars against the Ottomites.
235 Most humbly, therefore, bending to your state,
I crave fit disposition for my wife;
Due reference of place and exhibition;
With such accommodation and besort
As levels with her breeding.

**Duke**

                  If you please,
  Be't at her father's.

**Brabantio**

                      I'll not have it so.        240

**Othello**

  Nor I.

**Desdemona**

      Nor I. I would not there reside,
  To put my father in impatient thoughts
  By being in his eye. Most gracious Duke,
  To my unfolding lend your prosperous ear,
  And let me find a charter in your voice        245
  T' assist my simpleness.

**Duke**

  What would you, Desdemona?

**Desdemona**

      That I did love the Moor to live with him,    250
  My downright violence and storm of fortunes
  My trumpet to the world. My heart's subdu'd
  Even to the very quality of my lord:
  I saw Othello's visage in his mind;
  And to his honours and his valiant parts
  Did I my soul and fortunes consecrate.
  So that, dear lords, if I be left behind,       255
  A moth of peace, and he go to the war,
  The rites for why I love him are bereft me,
  And I a heavy interim shall support
  By his dear absence. Let me go with him.

**Othello**

  Let her have your voice.              260
  Vouch with me, heaven, I therefore beg it not
  To please the palate of my appetite;
  Nor to comply with heat – the young affects
  In me defunct – and proper satisfaction;
  But to be free and bounteous to her mind.    265
  And heaven defend your good souls that you think

I will your serious and great business scant
For she is with me. No, when light-wing'd toys
Of feather'd Cupid seel with wanton dullness
270 My speculative and offic'd instruments,
That my disports corrupt and taint my business,
Let huswives make a skillet of my helm,
And all indign and base adversities
Make head against my estimation!

*Duke*
275 Be it as you shall privately determine,
Either for her stay or going. Th' affair cries haste,
And speed must answer it. You must away to-night.

*Desdemona*
To-night, my lord!

*Duke*
                    This night.

*Othello*
                              With all my heart.

*Duke*
At nine i' th' morning here we'll meet again.
280 Othello, leave some officer behind,
And he shall our commission bring to you;
With such things else of quality and respect
As doth import you.

*Othello*
                    So please your Grace, my ancient;
A man he is of honesty and trust.
285 To his conveyance I assign my wife,
With what else needful your good Grace shall
    think
To be sent after me.

*Duke*
                    Let it be so.
Good night to every one. *[To* BRABANTIO*]* And, noble
    signior,
If virtue no delighted beauty lack,
290 Your son-in-law is far more fair than black.

**1 Senator**
    Adieu, brave Moor; use Desdemona well.
**Brabantio**
    Look to her, Moor, if thou hast eyes to see:
    She has deceiv'd her father, and may thee.

*[Exeunt DUKE, SENATORS, OFFICERS etc.]*

**Othello**
    My life upon her faith! – Honest Iago,
    My Desdemona must I leave to thee.                    295
    I prithee let thy wife attend on her;
    And bring them after in the best advantage.
    Come, Desdemona, I have but an hour
    Of love, of worldly matter and direction,
    To spend with thee. We must obey the time.            300

*[Exeunt OTHELLO and DESDEMONA.]*

**Roderigo**
    Iago!
**Iago**
    What say'st thou, noble heart?
**Roderigo**
    What will I do, thinkest thou?
**Iago**
    Why, go to bed and sleep.
**Roderigo**
    I will incontinently drown myself.                    305
**Iago**
    Well, if thou dost, I shall never love thee after it. Why,
    thou silly gentleman!
**Roderigo**
    It is silliness to live when to live is torment; and then
    have we a prescription to die when death is our
    physician.                                            310
**Iago**
    O villainous! I ha look'd upon the world for four times
    seven years; and since I could distinguish betwixt a

benefit and an injury, I never found a man that knew how to love himself. Ere I would say I would drown
315    myself for the love of a guinea-hen, I would change my humanity with a baboon.

*Roderigo*

What should I do? I confess it is my shame to be so fond, but it is not in my virtue to amend it.

*Iago*

Virtue? A fig! 'Tis in ourselves that we are thus or thus.
320    Our bodies are our gardens to the which our wills are gardeners; so that if we will plant nettles or sow lettuce, set hyssop and weed up thyme, supply it with one gender of herbs or distract it with many, either to have it sterile with idleness or manur'd with industry – why,
325    the power and corrigible authority of this lies in our wills. If the balance of our lives had not one scale of reason to poise another of sensuality, the blood and baseness of our natures would conduct us to most preposterous conclusions. But we have reason to cool
330    our raging motions, our carnal stings, our unbitted lusts; whereof I take this that you call love to be a sect or scion.

*Roderigo*

It cannot be.

*Iago*

It is merely a lust of the blood and a permission of
335    the will. Come, be a man. Drown thyself? Drown cats and blind puppies! I have profess'd me thy friend, and I confess me knit to thy deserving with cables of perdurable toughness. I could never better stead thee than now. Put money in thy purse; follow thou the
340    wars; defeat thy favour with an usurp'd beard. I say, put money in thy purse. It cannot be long that Desdemona should continue her love to the Moor – put money in thy purse – nor he his to her: it was a violent commencement in her, and thou shalt see an answer-
345    able sequestration – put but money in thy purse. These

Moors are changeable in their wills – fill thy purse with
money. The food that to him now is as luscious as
locusts shall be to him shortly as acerbe as the colo-
quintida. She must change for youth; when she is sated
with his body, she will find the error of her choice. 350
Therefore put money in thy purse. If thou wilt needs
damn thyself, do it a more delicate way than drowning.
Make all the money thou canst. If sanctimony and a
frail vow betwixt an erring barbarian and a super-subtle
Venetian be not too hard for my wits and all the tribe 325
of hell, thou shalt enjoy her; therefore make money.
A pox a drowning thyself! 'Tis clean out of the way.
Seek thou rather to be hang'd in compassing thy joy
than to be drown'd and go without her.

*Roderigo*

Wilt thou be fast to my hopes, if I depend on the 360
issue?

*Iago*

Thou art sure of me – go make money. I have told
thee often, and I retell thee again and again I hate the
Moor. My cause is hearted: thine hath no less reason.
Let us be conjunctive in our revenge against him. If 365
thou canst cuckold him, thou dost thyself a pleasure,
me a sport. There are many events in the womb of
time which will be delivered. Traverse; go; provide thy
money. We will have more of this to-morrow. Adieu.

*Roderigo*

Where shall we meet i' th' morning?                        370

*Iago*

At my lodging.

*Roderigo*

I'll be with thee betimes.

*Iago*

Go to; farewell. Do you hear, Roderigo?

*Roderigo*

What say you?

*Iago*

375     No more of drowning, do you hear?

*Roderigo*

I am chang'd.

*Iago*

Go to; farewell. Put money enough in your purse.

*Roderigo*

I'll sell all my land. *[Exit* RODERIGO.*]*

*Iago*

Thus do I ever make my fool my purse;

380     For I mine own gain'd knowledge should profane
If I would time expend with such a snipe
But for my sport and profit. I hate the Moor;
And it is thought abroad that 'twixt my sheets
'Has done my office. I know not if't be true;

385     Yet I, for mere suspicion in that kind,
Will do as if for surety. He holds me well;
The better shall my purpose work on him.
Cassio's a proper man. Let me see now:
To get his place, and to plume up my will

390     In double knavery. How, how? Let's see:
After some time to abuse Othello's ear
That he is too familiar with his wife.
He hath a person and a smooth dispose
To be suspected – fram'd to make women false.

395     The Moor is of a free and open nature
That thinks men honest that but seem to be so;
And will as tenderly be led by th' nose
As asses are.
I ha't – it is engender'd. Hell and night

400     Must bring this monstrous birth to the world's light.
         *[Exit.]*

# ACT TWO
## SCENE I

### Cyprus. A sea-port.

*[Enter MONTANO, Governor of Cyprus, with two other Gentlemen.]*

*Montano*
What from the cape can you discern at sea?
*1 Gentleman*
Nothing at all; it is a high-wrought flood.
I cannot 'twixt the heaven and the main
Descry a sail.
*Montano*
Methinks the wind hath spoke aloud at land;                    5
A fuller blast ne'er shook our battlements.
If it ha ruffian'd so upon the sea,
What ribs of oak, when mountains melt on them,
Can hold the mortise? What shall we hear of this?
*2 Gentleman*
A segregation of the Turkish fleet.                            10
For do but stand upon the banning shore,
The chidden billow seems to pelt the clouds;
The wind-shak'd surge, with high and monstrous
     mane,
Seems to cast water on the burning Bear,
And quench the guards of th' ever-fired pole.                  15
I never did like molestation view
On the enchafed flood.
*Montano*
                    If that the Turkish fleet
Be not enshelter'd and embay'd, they are drown'd:
It is impossible they bear it out.

*[Enter a third Gentleman.]*

*3 Gentleman*

20    News, lads! Your wars are done.
    The desperate tempest hath so bang'd the Turk
    That their designment halts. A noble ship of Venice
    Hath seen a grievous wreck and sufferance
    On most part of their fleet.

*Montano*

    How! Is this true?

*3 Gentleman*

25                The ship is here put in,
    A Veronesa; Michael Cassio,
    Lieutenant to the warlike Moor Othello,
    Is come ashore: the Moor himself at sea,
    And is in full commission here for Cyprus.

*Montano*

30    I am glad on't; 'tis a worthy governor.

*3 Gentleman*

    But this same Cassio, though he speak of comfort
    Touching the Turkish loss, yet he looks sadly
    And prays the Moor be safe; for they were parted
    With foul and violent tempest.

*Montano*

                    Pray heaven he be;

35    For I have serv'd him, and the man commands
    Like a full soldier. Let's to the sea-side, ho!
    As well to see the vessel that's come in
    As to throw out our eyes for brave Othello,
    Even till we make the main and th' aerial blue
    An indistinct regard.

*3 Gentleman*

40                Come, let's do so;
    For every minute is expectancy
    Of more arrivance.

*[Enter* CASSIO.*]*

*Cassio*

    Thanks you, the valiant of this war-like isle,

That so approve the Moor. O, let the heavens
Give him defence against their elements,                45
For I have lost him on a dangerous sea!
Montano
    Is he well shipp'd?
Cassio
    His bark is stoutly timber'd, and his pilot
    Of very expert and approv'd allowance;
    Therefore my hopes, not surfeited to death, Stand in
        bold cure.                                       50

            *[Within: A sail, a sail, a sail!]*

            *[Enter a Messenger.]*

Cassio
    What noise?
Messenger
    The town is empty; on the brow o' th' sea
    Stand ranks of people, and they cry 'A sail!'
Cassio
    My hopes do shape him for the Governor. *[A shot.]*
2 Gentleman
    They do discharge the shot of courtesy:              55
    Our friend at least.
Cassio
                    I pray you, sir, go forth,
    And give us truth who 'tis that is arriv'd.
2 Gentleman
    I shall. *[Exit.]*
Montano
    But, good Lieutenant, is your general wiv'd?
Cassio
    Most fortunately: he hath achiev'd a maid            60
    That paragons description and wild fame;
    One that excels the quirks of blazoning pens,
    And in th' essential vesture of creation
    Does tire the ingener.

*[Re-enter second Gentleman.]*

               Now, who has put in?

*2 Gentleman*

65    'Tis one Iago, ancient to the General.

*Cassio*

    'Has had most favourable and happy speed.
    Tempests themselves, high seas, and howling winds,
    The gutter'd rocks, and congregated sands,
    Traitors ensteep'd to enclog the guiltless keel,
70    As having sense of beauty, do omit
    Their mortal natures, letting go safely by
    The divine Desdemona.

*Montano*

                    What is she?

*Cassio*

    She that I spake of – our great Captain's Captain,
    Left in the conduct of the bold Iago;
75    Whose footing here anticipates our thoughts
    A se'nnight's speed. Great Jove, Othello guard,
    And swell his sail with thine own powerful breath,
    That he may bless this bay with his tall ship,
    Make love's quick pants in Desdemona's arms,
80    Give renew'd fire to our extinct spirits,
    And bring all Cyprus comfort!

*[Enter DESDEMONA, IAGO, EMILIA, RODERIGO, and Attendants.]*

                    O, behold,
    The riches of the ship is come ashore!
    Ye men of Cyprus, let her have your knees.
    Hall to thee, lady! and the grace of heaven,
85    Before, behind thee, and on every hand,
    Enwheel thee round!

*Desdemona*

                I thank you, valiant Cassio.
    What tidings can you tell me of my lord?

*Cassio*
   He is not yet arriv'd; nor know I aught
   But that he's well, and will be shortly here.
*Desdemona*
   O, but I fear! How lost you company?                    90
*Cassio*
   The great contention of the sea and skies
   Parted our fellowship.

                *[Within: A sail, a sail!]*

                But hark – 'A sail!' *[A shot.]*
*2 Gentleman*
   They give their greeting to the citadel:
   This likewise is a friend.
*Cassio*
                So speaks this voice.
   See for the news.       *[Exit Gentleman.]*           95
   Good ancient, you are welcome. *[To EMILIA]*
                           Welcome, mistress.
   Let it not gall your patience, good Iago,
   That I extend my manners; 'tis my breeding
   That gives me this bold show of courtesy.

                *[Kissing her.]*

*Iago*
   Sir, would she give you so much of her lips             100
   As of her tongue she oft bestows on me,
   You'd have enough.
*Desdemona*
   Alas, she has no speech!
*Iago*
                I know too much
   I find it aye when I ha list to sleep.
   Marry, before your ladyship, I grant,                   105
   She puts her tongue a little in her heart
   And chides with thinking.

*Emilia*
You ha little cause to say so.

*Iago*
Come on, come on; you are pictures out a-doors, bells
110   in your parlours, wildcats in your kitchens, saints in
your injuries, devils being offended, players in your
huswifery, and huswives in your beds.

*Desdemona*
O, fie upon thee, slanderer!

*Iago*
Nay, it is true, or else I am a Turk:
115   You rise to play, and go to bed to work.

*Emilia*
You shall not write my praise.

*Iago*
                    No, let me not.

*Desdemona*
What wouldst write of me if thou shouldst praise
    me?

*Iago*
O gentle lady, do not put me to't;
For I am nothing if not critical.

*Desdemona*
120   Come on, assay. – There's one gone to the harbour?

*Iago*
Ay, madam.

*Desdemona*
I am not merry; but I do beguile
The thing I am by seeming otherwise.
Come, how wouldst thou praise me?

*Iago*
125   I am about it; but, indeed, my invention comes from
my pate as birdlime does from frieze – it plucks out
brains and all. But my Muse labours, and thus she is
deliver'd:
If she be fair and wise – fairness and wit,
130   The one's for use, the other useth it.

*Desdemona*

Well prais'd. How if she be black and witty?

*Iago*

If she be black, and thereto have a wit,
She'll find a white that shall her blackness hit.

*Desdemona*

Worse and worse!

*Emilia*

How if fair and foolish?                                                  135

*Iago*

She never yet was foolish that was fair;
For even her folly help'd her to an heir.

*Desdemona*

These are old fond paradoxes to make fools laugh i'
th' alehouse. What miserable praise hast thou for her
that's foul and foolish?                                                  140

*Iago*

There's none so foul, and foolish thereunto,
But does foul pranks which fair and wise ones do.

*Desdemona*

O heavy ignorance! that praises the worst best. But
what praise couldst thou bestow on a deserving woman
indeed – one that, in the authority of her merits, did  145
justly put on the vouch of very malice itself?

*Iago*

She that was ever fair, and never proud;
Had tongue at will, and yet was never loud;
Never lack'd gold, and yet went never gay;
Fled from her wish, and yet said 'Now I may';            150
She that, being ang'red, her revenge being nigh,
Bade her wrong stay and her displeasure fly;
She that in wisdom never was so frail
To change the cod's head for the salmon's tail;
She that could think, and ne'er disclose her
    mind;                                                                     155
See suitors following, and not look behind:
She was a wight, if ever such wight were –

*Desdemona*

To do what?

*Iago*

To suckle fools and chronicle small beer.

*Desdemona*

160 O most lame and impotent conclusion! Do not learn of him, Emilia, though he be thy husband. How say you, Cassio? Is he not a most profane and liberal counsellor?

*Cassio*

He speaks home, madam. You may relish him more 165 in the soldier than in the scholar.

*Iago*

*[Aside]* He takes her by the palm.

Ay, well said, whisper. With as little a web as this will I ensnare as great a fly as Cassio. Ay, smile upon her, do; I will gyve thee in thine own courtship. You say 170 true; 'tis so, indeed. If such tricks as these strip you out of your lieutenantry, it had been better you had not kiss'd your three fingers so oft, which now again you are most apt to play the sir in. Very good; well kissed! and excellent courtesy! 'Tis so, indeed. Yet again 175 your fingers to your lips? Would they were clyster-pipes for your sake!

*[Trumpet within.]*

The Moor! I know his trumpet.

*Cassio*

'Tis truly so.

*Desdemona*

Let's meet him, and receive him.

*Cassio*

Lo, where he comes!

*[Enter* OTHELLO *and Attendants.]*

*Othello*

O my fair warrior!

*Desdemona*
                    My dear Othello!
*Othello*
    It gives me wonder great as my content          180
    To see you here before me. O my soul's joy!
    If after every tempest come such calms,
    May the winds blow till they have waken'd death,
    And let the labouring bark climb hills of seas
    Olympus-high and duck again as low            185
    As hell's from heaven. If it were now to die,
    'Twere now to be most happy; for I fear
    My soul hath her content so absolute
    That not another comfort like to this
    Succeeds in unknown fate.
*Desdemona*
                        The heavens forbid          190
    But that our loves and comforts should increase
    Even as our days do grow!
*Othello*
                        Amen to that, sweet powers!
    I cannot speak enough of this content;
    It stops me here; it is too much of joy.
    And this, and this, the greatest discords be     195

                    *[They kiss.]*

    That e'er our hearts shall make!
*Iago*
    *[Aside]* O, you are well tun'd now!
    But I'll set down the pegs that make this music,
    As honest as I am.
*Othello*
                    Come, let us to the castle.
    News, friends: our wars are done; the Turks are
        drown'd.                                      200
    How do our old acquaintance of the isle?
    Honey, you shall be well desir'd in Cyprus;
    I have found great love amongst them. O my sweet,

I prattle out of fashion, and I dote
205   In mine own comforts. I prithee, good Iago,
Go to the bay, and disembark my coffers;
Bring thou the Master to the Citadel;
He is a good one, and his worthiness
Does challenge much respect. Come, Desdemona,
210   Once more well met at Cyprus.

*[Exeunt all but* IAGO *and* RODERIGO.*]*

*Iago*

*[To one leaving]* Do thou meet me presently at the
harbour. *[To* RODERIGO*]* Come hither. If thou be'st
valiant – as they say base men being in love have then
a nobility in their natures more than is native to them
215   – list me. The Lieutenant to-night watches on the court
of guard. First, I must tell thee this: Desdemona is
directly in love with him.

*Roderigo*

With him! Why, 'tis not possible.

*Iago*

Lay thy finger thus, and let thy soul be instructed. Mark
220   me with what violence she first lov'd the Moor, but
for bragging and telling her fantastical lies. To love him
still for prating? – let not thy discreet heart think it.
Her eye must be fed; and what delight shall she have
to look on the devil? When the blood is made dull
225   with the act of sport, there should be – again to inflame
it, and to give satiety a fresh appetite – loveliness in
favour, sympathy in years, manners, and beauties – all
which the Moor is defective in. Now for want of these
requir'd conveniences, her delicate tenderness will find
230   itself abus'd, begin to heave the gorge, disrelish and
abhor the Moor; very nature will instruct her in it, and
compel her to some second choice. Now, sir, this
granted – as it is a most pregnant and unforc'd position
– who stands so eminent in the degree of this fortune
235   as Cassio does? A knave very voluble; no further

conscionable than in putting on the mere form of civil
and humane seeming, for the better compassing of his
salt and most hidden loose affection? Why, none; why,
none. A slipper and subtle knave; a finder-out of occasion; that has an eye can stamp and counterfeit 240
advantages, though true advantage never present itself;
a devilish knave! Besides, the knave is handsome,
young, and hath all those requisites in him that folly
and green minds look after; a pestilent complete knave,
and the woman hath found him already. 245

*Roderigo*

I cannot believe that in her; she's full of most blest
condition.

*Iago*

Blest fig's end! The wine she drinks is made of grapes.
If she had been blest, she would never have lov'd the
Moor. Blest pudding! Didst thou not see her paddle 250
with the palm of his hand? Didst not mark that?

*Roderigo*

Yes, that I did; but that was but courtesy.

*Iago*

Lechery, by this hand; an index and obscure prologue
to the history of lust and foul thoughts. They met so
near with their lips that their breaths embrac'd 255
together. Villainous thoughts, Roderigo! When these
mutualities so marshal the way, hard at hand comes
the master and main exercise, th' incorporate conclusion. Pish! But, sir, be you rul'd by me; I have brought
you from Venice. Watch you to-night; for your 260
command, I'll lay't upon you. Cassio knows you not;
I'll not be far from you. Do you find some occasion
to anger Cassio, either by speaking too loud, or tainting
his discipline, or from what other course you please,
which the time shall more favourably minister. 265

*Roderigo*

Well.

*Iago*

Sir, he's rash, and very sudden in choler, and haply
with his truncheon may strike at you; provoke him
that he may; for even out of that will I cause these of
270   Cyprus to mutiny, whose qualification shall come into
no true taste again but by the displanting of Cassio.
So shall you have a shorter journey to your desires by
the means I shall then have to prefer them; and the
impediment most profitably remov'd, without the
275   which there were no expectation of our prosperity.

*Roderigo*

I will do this, if you can bring it to any opportunity.

*Iago*

I warrant thee. Meet me by and by at the citadel.
I must fetch his necessaries ashore. Farewell.

*Roderigo*

Adieu. *[Exit.]*

*Iago*

280   That Cassio loves her, I do well believe it;
That she loves him, 'tis apt and of great credit.
The Moor, howbeit that I endure him not,
Is of a constant, loving, noble nature;
And I dare think he'll prove to Desdemona
285   A most dear husband. Now I do love her too;
Not out of absolute lust, though per-adventure
I stand accountant for as great a sin,
But partly led to diet my revenge,
For that I do suspect the lustful Moor
290   Hath leap'd into my seat; the thought whereof
Doth like a poisonous mineral gnaw my inwards;
And nothing can nor shall content my soul
Till I am even'd with him, wife for wife;
Or failing so, yet that I put the Moor
295   At least into a jealousy so strong
That judgment cannot cure. Which thing to do,
If this poor trash of Venice, whom I trash
For his quick hunting, stand the putting on,

I'll have our Michael Cassio on the hip,
Abuse him to the Moor in the rank garb –                    300
For I fear Cassio with my night-cap too;
Make the Moor thank me, love me, and reward me,
For making him egregiously an ass,
And practising upon his peace and quiet
Even to madness. 'Tis here, but yet confus'd:              305
Knavery's plain face is never seen till us'd.

*[Exit.]*

## SCENE II

*Cyprus. A street.*

*[Enter* OTHELLO*'s Herald with a proclamation; People following.]*

Herald

It is Othello's pleasure, our noble and valiant general,
that, upon certain tidings now arriv'd, importing the
mere perdition of the Turkish fleet, every man put
himself into triumph; some to dance, some to make
5    bonfires, each man to what sport and revels his addic-
tion leads him; for, besides these beneficial news, it is
the celebration of his nuptial. So much was his pleasure
should be proclaimed. All offices are open; and there
is full liberty of feasting from this present hour of five
10   till the bell have told eleven. Heaven bless the isle of
Cyprus and our noble general Othello! *[Exeunt.]*

# SCENE III

*Cyprus. The citadel.*

*[Enter* OTHELLO, DESDEMONA, CASSIO, *and Attendants.]*

**Othello**
Good Michael, look you to the guard to-night.
Let's teach ourselves that honourable stop,
Not to outsport discretion.

**Cassio**
Iago hath direction what to do;
But, notwithstanding, with my personal eye                    5
Will I look to't.

**Othello**
                               Iago is most honest.
Michael, good night. To-morrow with your earliest
Let me have speech with you. *[To* DESDEMONA*]*
                               Come, my dear love,
The purchase made, the fruits are to ensue;
That profit's yet to come twixt me and you. –         10
Good night. *[Exeunt* OTHELLO, DESDEMONA *and Attendants.]*

*[Enter* IAGO.*]*

**Cassio**
Welcome, Iago; we must to the watch.

**Iago**
Not this hour, Lieutenant; 'tis not yet ten a clock. Our
general cast us thus early for the love of his Desdemona;
who let us not therefore blame. He hath not yet made    15
wanton the night with her; and she is sport for Jove.

**Cassio**
She is a most exquisite lady.

**Iago**
And, I'll warrant her, full of game.

49

*Cassio*

Indeed, she is a most fresh and delicate creature.

*Iago*

What an eye she has! Methinks it sounds a parley to
20    provocation.

*Cassio*

An inviting eye; and yet methinks right modest.

*Iago*

And when she speaks, is it not an alarm to love?

*Cassio*

She is indeed perfection.

*Iago*

Well, happiness to their sheets! Come, Lieutenant, I
25    have a stoup of wine; and here without are a brace of
Cyprus gallants that would fain have a measure to the
health of the black Othello.

*Cassio*

Not to-night, good Iago. I have very poor and unhappy
brains for drinking; I could well wish courtesy would
30    invent some other custom of entertainment.

*Iago*

O, they are our friends – but one cup; I'll drink for
you.

*Cassio*

I have drunk but one cup to-night, and that was craftily
qualified too, and behold what innovation it makes
35    here. I am unfortunate in the infirmity, and dare not
task my weakness with any more.

*Iago*

What man! 'Tis a night of revels. The gallants desire
it.

*Cassio*

Where are they?

*Iago*

40    Here at the door; I pray you call them in.

*Cassio*

I'll do't; but it dislikes me. *[Exit.]*

*Iago*
    If I can fasten but one cup upon him,
    With that which he hath drunk to-night already,
    He'll be as full of quarrel and offence
    As my young mistress' dog. Now my sick fool Roderigo,     45
    Whom love hath turn'd almost the wrong side outward,
    To Desdemona hath to-night carous'd
    Potations pottle deep; and he's to watch.
    Three else of Cyprus – noble swelling spirits,
    That hold their honours in a wary distance,     50
    The very elements of this warlike isle –
    Have I to-night fluster'd with flowing cups,
    And they watch too. Now, 'mongst this flock of drunkards
    Am I to put our Cassio in some action
    That may offend the isle – but here they come.     55

    *[Re-enter* CASSIO *with* MONTANO, *and Gentlemen,*
    *followed by Servant with wine.]*

    If consequence do but approve my dream,
    My boat sails freely, both with wind and stream.
*Cassio*
    Fore God, they have given me a rouse already.
*Montano*
    Good faith, a little one; not past a pint, as I am a soldier.     60
*Iago*
    Some wine, ho!
    *[Sings]* And let me the canakin clink, clink;

        And let me the canakin clink.
        A soldier's a man;
        O, man's life's but a span;     65
        Why, then, let a soldier drink –

    Some wine, boys.

*Cassio*
Fore God, an excellent song!

*Iago*
70 I learn'd it in England, where indeed they are most potent in potting: your Dane, your German, and your swag-bellied Hollander – Drink, ho! – are nothing to your English.

*Cassio*
Is your Englishman so expert in his drinking?

*Iago*
75 Why, he drinks you with facility your Dane dead drunk; he sweats not to overthrow your Almain; he gives your Hollander a vomit ere the next pottle can be fill'd.

*Cassio*
To the health of our General!

*Montano*
I am for it, Lieutenant; and I'll do you justice.

*Iago*
O sweet England! *[Sings.]*

80     King Stephen was and a worthy peer,
        His breeches cost him but a crown;
    He held 'em sixpence all too dear,
        With that he call'd the tailor lown.
    He was a wight of high renown,
85         And thou art but of low degree.
    'Tis pride that pulls the country down;
        Then take thy auld cloak about thee –

Some wine, ho!

*Cassio*
Fore God, this is a more exquisite song than the other.

*Iago*
90 Will you hear't again?

*Cassio*
No; for I hold him to be unworthy of his place that does those things. Well, God's above all; and there be souls must be saved, and there be souls must not be saved.

*Iago*

It's true, good Lieutenant.

*Cassio*

For mine own part – no offence to the                                    95
General, nor any man of quality – I hope to be
   saved.

*Iago*

And so do I too, Lieutenant.

*Cassio*

Ay, but, by your leave, not before me; the Lieutenant
is to be saved before the Ancient. Let's have no more
of this; let's to our affairs. God forgive us our sins. 100
Gentlemen, let's look to our business. Do not think,
gentlemen, I am drunk. This is my ancient; this is my
right hand, and this is my left hand. I am not drunk
now; I can stand well enough, and I speak well enough.

*All*

Excellent well.                                                         105

*Cassio*

Why, very well, then. You must not think, then, that
I am drunk. *[Exit.]*

*Montano*

To the platform, masters; come, let's set the watch.

*Iago*

You see this fellow that is gone before:
He is a soldier fit to stand by Caesar
And give direction; and do but see his vice;              110
'Tis to his virtue a just equinox,
The one as long as th' other. 'Tis pity of him.
I fear the trust Othello puts him in,
On some odd time of his infirmity,                       115
Will shake this island.

*Montano*

                            But is he often thus?

*Iago*

'Tis evermore the prologue to his sleep:
He'll watch the horologe a double set,

If drink rock not his cradle.

*Monatno*

It were well

120   The General were put in mind of it.
Perhaps he sees it not, or his good nature
Prizes the virtue that appears in Cassio,
And looks not on his evils. Is not this true?

*[Enter* RODERIGO.*]*

*Iago*

*[Aside to him]* How, now, Roderigo!

125   I pray you, after the Lieutenant; go.

*[Exit* RODERIGO.*]*

*Montano*

And 'tis great pity that the noble Moor
Should hazard such a place as his own second
With one of an ingraft infirmity:
It were an honest action to say
So to the Moor.

*Iago*

Not I, for this fair island;

130   I do love Cassio well; and would do much
To cure him of this evil.

*[Within: Help, help!]*

But hark, what noise?

*[Re-enter* CASSIO, *driving in* RODERIGO.*]*

*Cassio*

Zounds, you rogue, you rascal!

*Montano*

135   What's the matter, Lieutenant?

*Cassio*

A knave teach me my duty! But I'll beat the knave into
a twiggen bottle.

*Roderigo*
  Beat me!
*Cassio*
  Dost thou prate, rogue? *[Strikes him.]*
*Montano*
  Nay, good Lieutenant; I pray you, sir, hold your hand.  140
*Cassio*
  Let me go, sir, or I'll knock you o'er the mazard.
*Montano*
  Come, come, you're drunk.
*Cassio*
  Drunk! *[They fight.]*
*Iago*
  *[Aside to* RODERIGO*]* Away, I say!
  Go out and cry a mutiny. *[Exit* RODERIGO.*]*
  Nay, good Lieutenant. God's will, gentlemen!          145
  Help, ho! – Lieutenant – sir – Montano – sir –
  Help, masters! Here's a goodly watch indeed!

  *[A bell rung.]*

  Who's that which rings the bell? Diablo, ho!
  The town will rise. God's will, Lieutenant, hold.
  You'll be asham'd for ever.                           150

  *[Re-enter OTHELLO and Gentlemen, with weapons.]*

*Othello*
  What is the matter here?
*Montano*
  Zounds, I bleed still; I am hurt to the death – He dies.
*Othello*
  Hold, for your lives!
*Iago*
  Hold, ho! Lieutenant – sir – Montano – gentlemen –
  Have you forgot all sense of place and duty?          155
  Hold! The General speaks to you; hold, hold, for
      shame!

*Othello*

Why, how now, ho! From whence ariseth this?
Are we turn'd Turks, and to ourselves do that
Which Heaven hath forbid the Ottomites?
160   For Christian shame, put by this barbarous brawl.
He that stirs next to carve for his own rage
Holds his soul light: he dies upon his motion.
Silence that dreadful bell; it frights the isle
From her propriety. What's the matter, masters?
165   Honest Iago, that looks dead with grieving,
Speak. Who began this? On thy love, I charge thee.

*Iago*

I do not know. Friends all but now, even now,
In quarter, and in terms, like bride and groom
Divesting them for bed; and then, but now,
170   As if some planet had unwitted men,
Swords out, and tilting one at other's breast
In opposition bloody. I cannot speak
Any beginning to this peevish odds;
And would in action glorious I had lost
175   These legs that brought me to a part of it!

*Othello*

How comes it, Michael, you are thus forgot?

*Cassio*

I pray you, pardon me; I cannot speak.

*Othello*

Worthy Montano, you were wont be civil;
The gravity and stillness of your youth
180   The world hath noted, and your name is great
In mouths of wisest censure – what's the matter
That you unlace your reputation thus,
And spend your rich opinion for the name
Of a night-brawler? Give me answer to't.

*Montano*

185   Worthy Othello, I am hurt to danger;
Your officer Iago can inform you,
While I spare speech, which something now offends
     me,

Of all that I do know; nor know I aught
By me that's said or done amiss this night,
Unless self-charity be sometimes a vice,                    190
And to defend ourselves it be a sin
When violence assails us.

**Othello**

      Now, by heaven,
My blood begins my safer guides to rule;
And passion, having my best judgment collied,
Assays to lead the way. Zounds if I stir                    195
Or do but lift this arm, the best of you
Shall sink in my rebuke. Give me to know
How this foul rout began, who set it on;
And he that is approv'd in this offence,
Though he had twinn'd with me, both at a birth,             200
Shall lose me. What! in a town of war,
Yet wild, the people's hearts brim full of fear,
To manage private and domestic quarrel,
In night, and on the court and guard of safety!
'Tis monstrous. Iago, who began't?                          205

**Montano**

If partially affin'd, or leagu'd in office,
Thou dost deliver more or less than truth,
Thou art no soldier.

**Iago**

      Touch me not so near;
I had rather ha this tongue cut from my mouth
Than it should do offence to Michael Cassio;                210
Yet, I persuade myself, to speak the truth
Shall nothing wrong him. This it is, General.
Montano and myself being in speech,
There comes a fellow crying out for help,
And Cassio following him with determin'd sword              215
To execute upon him. Sir, this gentleman
Steps in to Cassio and entreats his pause;
Myself the crying fellow did pursue,
Lest by his clamour, as it so fell out,

220 The town might fall in fright; he, swift of foot,
Outran my purpose, and I return'd the rather
For that I heard the clink and fall of swords,
And Cassio high in oath; which till to-night
I ne'er might see before. When I came back,
230 For this was brief, I found them close together
At blow and thrust, even as again they were
When you yourself did part them.
More of this matter can I not report;
But men are men; the best sometimes forget.
235 Though Cassio did some little wrong to him,
As men in rage strike those that wish them best,
Yet surely Cassio, I believe, receiv'd
From him that fled some strange indignity
Which patience could not pass.

*Othello*

                           I know, Iago,
240 Thy honesty and love doth mince this matter,
Making it light to Cassio. Cassio, I love thee;
But never more be officer of mine.

*[Re-enter DESDEMONA, attended.]*

Look if my gentle love be not rais'd up.
I'll make thee an example.

*Desdemona*

What is the matter, dear?

*Othello*

245                         All's well now, sweeting;
Come away to bed. *[To MONTANO]* Sir, for your hurts,
Myself will be your surgeon. Lead him off.

*[MONTANO is led off.]*

Iago, look with care about the town,
And silence those whom this vile brawl distracted.
250 Come, Desdemona; 'tis the soldiers' life
To have their balmy slumbers wak'd with strife.

*[Exeunt all but IAGO and CASSIO.]*

*Iago*

What, are you hurt, Lieutenant?

*Cassio*

Ay, past all surgery.

*Iago*

Marry, God forbid!

*Cassio*

Reputation, reputation, reputation! O, I have lost my 250
reputation! I have lost the immortal part of myself,
and what remains is bestial. My reputation, Iago, my
reputation!

*Iago*

As I am an honest man, I had thought you had receiv'd
some bodily wound; there is more sense in that than 255
in reputation. Reputation is an idle and most false
imposition; oft got without merit, and lost without
deserving. You have lost no reputation at all, unless
you repute yourself such a loser. What, man! there are
more ways to recover the General again; you are but 260
now cast in his mood, a punishment more in policy
than in malice; even so as one would beat his offence-
less dog to affright an imperious lion. Sue to him again,
and he's yours.

*Cassio*

I will rather sue to be despis'd than to deceive so good 265
a commander with so slight, so drunken, and so indis-
creet an officer. Drunk! And speak parrot! And squabble,
swagger, swear! And discourse fustian with one's own
shadow! O thou invisible spirit of wine, if thou hast
no name to be known by, let us call thee devil! 270

*Iago*

What was he that you follow'd with your sword? What
had he done to you?

*Cassio*

I know not.

*Iago*

Is't possible?

*Cassio*

275    I remember a mass of things, but nothing distinctly; a quarrel, but nothing wherefore. O God, that men should put an enemy in their mouths to steal away their brains! That we should with joy, pleasance, revel and applause, transform ourselves into beasts!

*Iago*

280    Why, but you are now well enough. How come you thus recovered?

*Cassio*

It hath pleas'd the devil drunkenness to give place to the devil wrath. One unperfectness shows me another, to make me frankly despise myself.

*Iago*

285    Come, you are too severe a moraller. As the time, the place, and the condition of this country stands, I could heartily wish this had not so befall'n; but since it is as it is, mend it for your own good.

*Cassio*

I will ask him for my place again: he shall tell me I
290    am a drunkard. Had I as many mouths as Hydra, such an answer would stop them all. To be now a sensible man, by and by a fool, and presently a beast! O strange! Every inordinate cup is unblest, and the ingredience is a devil.

*Iago*

295    Come, come, good wine is a good familiar creature if it be well us'd; exclaim no more against it. And, good Lieutenant, I think you think I love you.

*Cassio*

I have well approv'd it, sir. I drunk!

*Iago*

You or any man living may be drunk at a time, man.
300    I'll tell you what you shall do. Our General's wife is now the General – I may say so in this respect, for that he hath devoted and given up himself to the contemplation, mark, and denotement, of her parts

and graces – confess yourself freely to her; importune
her help to put you in your place again: she is of so 305
free, so kind, so apt, so blessed a disposition, she holds
it a vice in her goodness not to do more than she is
requested. This broken joint between you and her
husband entreat her to splinter; and, my fortunes
against any lay worth naming, this crack of your love 310
shall grow stronger than it was before.

*Cassio*

You advise me well.

*Iago*

I protest, in the sincerity of love and honest
kindness.

*Cassio*

I think it freely; and betimes in the morning I will 315
beseech the virtuous Desdemona to undertake for me.
I am desperate of my fortunes if they check me here.

*Iago*

You are in the right. Good night, Lieutenant; I must
    to the watch.

*Cassio*

Good night, honest Iago. *[Exit.]*                          320

*Iago*

And what's he, then, that says I play the villain?
When this advice is free I give and honest,
Probal to thinking, and indeed the course
To win the Moor again? For 'tis most easy
The inclining Desdemona to subdue                          325
In any honest suit: she's fram'd as fruitful
As the free elements. And then for her
To win the Moor – were't to renounce his baptism,
All seals and symbols of redeemed sin –
His soul is so enfetter'd to her love                      330
That she may make, unmake, do what she list,
Even as her appetite shall play the god
With his weak function. How am I, then, a villain
To counsel Cassio to this parallel course,

335    Directly to his good? Divinity of hell!
      When devils will their blackest sins put on,
      They do suggest at first with heavenly shows,
      As I do now; for whiles this honest fool
      Plies Desdemona to repair his fortunes,
340    And she for him pleads strongly to the Moor,
      I'll pour this pestilence into his ear –
      That she repeals him for her body's lust;
      And by how much she strives to do him good
      She shall undo her credit with the Moor.
345    So will I turn her virtue into pitch;
      And out of her own goodness make the net
      That shall enmesh them all.

*[Enter RODERIGO.]*

                      How now, Roderigo!

*Roderigo*
      I do follow here in the chase, not like a hound that
      hunts, but one that fills up the cry. My money is almost
350    spent; I have been to-night exceedingly well cudgell'd;
      and I think the issue will be – I shall have so much
      experience for my pains as that comes to; and so, with
      no money at all, and a little more wit, return again to
      Venice.

*Iago*
355    How poor are they that have not patience!
      What wound did ever heal but by degrees?
      Thou know'st we work by wit, and not by
          witchcraft;
      And wit depends on dilatory time.
      Doesn't not go well? Cassio hath beaten thee,
360    And thou, by that small hurt, hast cashier'd Cassio.
      Though other things grow fair against the sun,
      Yet fruits that blossom first will first be ripe.
      Content thyself awhile. By th' mass, 'tis morning!
      Pleasure and action make the hours seem short.
365    Retire thee; go where thou art billeted.

Away, I say; thou shalt know more here-after.
Nay, get thee gone. *[Exit* RODERIGO.*]*
Two things are to be done:
My wife must move for Cassio to her mistress;
I'll set her on;                                  370
Myself awhile to draw the Moor apart
And bring him jump when he may Cassio find
Soliciting his wife. Ay, that's the way;
Dull not device by coldness and delay. *[Exit.]*

# ACT THREE
## SCENE I

*Cyprus. Before the citadel.*

*[Enter CASSIO, with Musicians.]*

Cassio
> Masters, play here; I will content your pains.
> Something that's brief; and bid 'Good morrow,
>     General'. *[Music.]*

*[Enter Clown.]*

Clown
> Why masters, ha your instruments been in Naples, that
> they speak i' th' nose thus?
1 Musician
5   How, sir, how?
Clown
> Are these, I pray, call'd wind instruments?
1 Musician
> Ay, marry, are they, sir.
Clown
> O, thereby hangs a tail.
1 Musician
> Whereby hangs a tale, sir?
Clown
10   Marry, sir, by many a wind instrument that I know.
> But, masters, here's money for you; and the General
> so likes your music that he desires you, of all loves, to
> make no more noise with it.
1 Musician
> Well, sir, we will not.
Clown
15   If you have any music that may not be heard, to't
> again; but, as they say, to hear music the General does

not greatly care.

**1 Musician**

We have none such, sir.

**Clown**

Then put up your pipes in your bag, for I'll away. Go;
vanish into air; away.                                         20

*[Exeunt Musicians.]*

**Cassio**

Dost thou hear, my honest friend?

**Clown**

No, I hear not your honest friend; I hear you.

**Cassio**

Prithee keep up thy quillets. There's a poor piece of
gold for thee. If the gentlewoman that attends the
General's wife be stirring, tell her there's one Cassio   25
entreats her a little favour of speech. Wilt thou do
this?

**Clown**

She is stirring, sir; if she will stir hither, I shall seem
to notify unto her.

**Cassio**

Do, good my friend.    *[Exit Clown.]*

*[Enter IAGO.]*

In happy time, Iago.                       30

**Iago**

You have not been abed, then?

**Cassio**

Why, no; the day had broke before we parted.
I have made bold, Iago,
To send in to your wife: my suit to her
Is that she will to virtuous Desdemona                      35
Procure me some access.

**Iago**

I'll send her to you presently;
And I'll devise a mean to draw the Moor

Out of the way, that your converse and business
May be more free.

Cassio

40    I humbly thank you for't. *[Exit* IAGO*]* I never knew
A Florentine more kind and honest.

*[Enter* EMILIA.*]*

Emilia

Good morrow, good Lieutenant. I am sorry
For your displeasure; but all will sure be well.
The General and his wife are talking of it;
45    And she speaks for you stoutly: the Moor replies
That he you hurt is of great fame in Cyprus
And great affinity, and that in wholesome wisdom
He might not but refuse you; but he protests he
        loves you,
And needs no other suitor but his likings
50    To take the safest occasion by the front
To bring you in again.

Cassio

                        Yet, I beseech you,
If you think fit, or that it may be done,
Give me advantage of some brief discourse
With Desdemona alone.

Emilia

                        Pray you come in.
55    I will bestow you where you shall have time
To speak your bosom freely.

Cassio

                        I am much bound to you.

*[Exeunt.]*

# SCENE II

*Cyprus. The citadel.*

*[Enter* OTHELLO, IAGO, *and Gentlemen.]*

**Othello**
These letters give, Iago, to the pilot;
And by him do my duties to the Senate.
That done, I will be walking on the works;
Repair there to me.

**Iago**
                Well, my good lord, I'll do't.

**Othello**
This fortification, gentlemen – shall we see't?     5

**Gentleman**
We'll wait upon your lordship.

*[Exeunt.]*

# SCENE III

### Cyprus. The garden of the citadel.

*[Enter DESDEMONA, CASSIO, and EMILIA.]*

**Desdemona**
 Be thou assur'd, good Cassio, I will do
 All my abilities in thy behalf.
**Emilia**
 Good madam, do. I warrant it grieves my husband
 As if the case were his.
**Desdemona**
5 O, that's an honest fellow. Do not doubt, Cassio,
 But I will have my lord and you again
 As friendly as you were.
**Cassio**
       Bounteous madam,
 Whatever shall become of Michael Cassio,
 He's never any thing but your true servant.
**Desdemona**
10 I know't – I thank you. You do love my lord;
 You have known him long; and be you well assur'd
 He shall in strangeness stand no farther off
 Than in a politic distance.
**Cassio**
       Ay, but, lady,
 That policy may either last so long,
15 Or feed upon such nice and waterish diet,
 Or breed itself so out of circumstances,
 That, I being absent, and my place supplied,
 My general will forget my love and service.
**Desdemona**
 Do not doubt that; before Emilia here
20 I give thee warrant of thy place. Assure thee,
 If I do vow a friendship, I'll perform it
 To the last article. My lord shall never rest;
 I'll watch him tame, and talk him out of patience;

His bed shall seem a school, his board a shrift;
I'll intermingle everything he does                                    25
With Cassio's suit. Therefore be merry, Cassio;
For thy solicitor shall rather die
Than give thy cause away.

*[Enter* OTHELLO *and* IAGO.]

*Emilia*
Madam, here comes my lord.
*Cassio*
Madam, I'll take my leave.                                             30
*Desdemona*
Why, stay, and hear me speak.
*Cassio*
Madam, not now. I am very ill at ease,
Unfit for mine own purposes.
*Desdemona*
Well, do your discretion.

*[Exit* CASSIO.]

*Iago*
Ha! I like not that.
*Othello*
                         What dost thou say?                           35
*Iago*
Nothing, my lord; or if – I know not what.
*Othello*
Was not that Cassio parted from my wife?
*Iago*
Cassio, my lord! No, sure, I cannot think it,
That he would sneak away so guilty-like,
Seeing your coming.
*Othello*
                         I do believe 'twas he.                        40
*Desdemona*
How now, my lord!
I have been talking with a suitor here,

A man that languishes in your displeasure.

*Othello*

Who is't you mean?

*Desdemona*

45     Why, your lieutenant, Cassio. Good my lord,
If I have any grace or power to move you,
His present reconciliation take;
For if he be not one that truly loves you,
That errs in ignorance, and not in cunning,
50     I have no judgment in an honest face.
I prithee call him back.

*Othello*

                Went he hence now?

*Desdemona*

Yes, faith; so humbled
That he hath left part of his grief with me
To suffer with him. Good love, call him back.

*Othello*

55     Not now, sweet Desdemona; some other time.

*Desdemona*

But shall't be shortly?

*Othello*

                The sooner, sweet, for you.

*Desdemona*

Shall't be to-night at supper?

*Othello*

                No, not to-night.

*Desdemona*

To-morrow dinner, then?

*Othello*

                I shall not dine at home;
I meet the captains at the citadel.

*Desdemona*

60     Why, then, to-morrow night, or Tuesday morn,
On Tuesday noon or night, on Wednesday morn.
I prithee name the time; but let it not
Exceed three days. I'faith, he's penitent;

And yet his trespass, in our common reason –
Save that, they say, the wars must make example        65
Out of her best – is not almost a fault
T' incur a private check. When shall he come?
Tell me, Othello – I wonder in my soul
What you would ask me that I should deny,
Or stand so mamm'ring on. What! Michael Cassio,        70
That came a-wooing with you, and so many a time,
When I have spoke of you dispraisingly,
Hath ta'en your part – to have so much to do
To bring him in! By'r Lady, I could do much –
*Othello*
Prithee, no more; let him come when he will;        75
I will deny thee nothing.
*Desdemona*
                    Why, this is not a boon;
'Tis as I should entreat you wear your gloves,
Or feed on nourishing dishes, or keep you warm,
Or sue to you to do a peculiar profit
To your own person. Nay, when I have a suit        80
Wherein I mean to touch your love indeed,
It shall be full of poise and difficult weight,
And fearful to be granted.
*Othello*
                    I will deny thee nothing.
Whereon I do beseech thee grant me this,
To leave me but a little to myself.        85
*Desdemona*
Shall I deny you? No; farewell, my lord.
*Othello*
Farewell, my Desdemona. I'll come to thee straight.
*Desdemona*
Emilia, come. – Be as your fancies teach you;
Whate'er you be, I am obedient.

*[Exeunt* DESDEMONA *and* EMILIA.*]*

*Othello*
90    Excellent wretch! Perdition catch my soul
      But I do love thee; and when I love thee not
      Chaos is come again.
*Iago*
      My noble lord!
*Othello*
                          What dost thou say, Iago?
*Iago*
      Did Michael Cassio, when you woo'd my lady,
95    Know of your love?
*Othello*
      He did, from first to last. Why dost thou ask?
*Iago*
      But for a satisfaction of my thought – No further
      harm.
*Othello*
                Why of thy thought, Iago?
*Iago*
      I did not think he had been acquainted with her.
*Othello*
100   O, yes; and went between us very often.
*Iago*
      Indeed!
*Othello*
      Indeed? Ay, indeed. Discern'st thou aught in that?
      Is he not honest?
*Iago*
                          Honest, my lord?
*Othello*
      Honest? Ay, honest.
*Iago*
                          My lord, for aught I know.
*Othello*
      What dost thou think?
*Iago*
105                         Think, my lord?

*Othello*

    Think, my lord! By-heaven, he echoes me,
    As if there were some monster in his thought
    Too hideous to be shown. Thou dost mean
        something:
    I heard thee say but now thou lik'st not that,
    When Cassio left my wife. What didst not like?    110
    And when I told thee he was of my counsel
    In my whole course of wooing, thou criedst
        'Indeed!'
    And didst contract and purse thy brow together,
    As if thou then hadst shut up in thy brain
    Some horrible conceit. If thou dost love me,    115
    Show me thy thought.

*Iago*

    My lord, you know I love you.

*Othello*

                      I think thou dost;
    And for I know thou art full of love and honesty,
    And weigh'st thy words before thou giv'st them
        breath,
    Therefore these stops of thine affright me the more;    120
    For such things in a false disloyal knave
    Are tricks of custom; but in a man that's just
    They are close delations, working from the heart
    That passion cannot rule.

*Iago*

                  For Michael Cassio,
    I dare presume I think that he is honest.    125

*Othello*

    I think so too.

*Iago*

              Men should be that they seem;
    Or those that be not, would they might seem none!

*Othello*

    Certain, men should be what they seem.

*Iago*
> Why then, I think Cassio's an honest man.

*Othello*
130 Nay, yet there's more in this.
> I prithee speak to me as to thy thinkings,
> As thou dost ruminate; and give thy worst of
>     thoughts
> The worst of words.

*Iago*
>                    Good my lord, pardon me.
> Though I am bound to every act of duty,
135 I am not bound to that all slaves are free to –
> Utter my thoughts. Why, say they are vile and false,
> As where's that palace whereinto foul things
> Sometimes intrude not? Who has that breast so pure
> But some uncleanly apprehensions
140 Keep leets and law-days, and in sessions sit
> With meditations lawful?

*Othello*
> Thou dost conspire against thy friend, Iago,
> If thou but think'st him wrong'd, and mak'st his ear
> A stranger to thy thoughts.

*Iago*
>                    I do beseech you,
145 Though I perchance am vicious in my guess,
> As, I confess, it is my nature's plague
> To spy into abuses, and oft my jealousy
> Shapes faults that are not – that your wisdom
> From one that so imperfectly conjects,
150 Would take no notice; nor build yourself a trouble.
> Out of his scattering and unsure observance.
> It were not for your quiet nor your good,
> Nor for my manhood, honesty, or wisdom,
5 To let you know my thoughts.

*Othello*
155 Zounds! What dost thou mean?

*Iago*
    Good name in man and woman, dear my lord,
    Is the immediate jewel of their souls:
    Who steals my purse steals trash; 'tis something,
        nothing;
    'Twas mine, 'tis his, and has been slave to
        thousands;
    But he that filches from me my good name      160
    Robs me of that which not enriches him
    And makes me poor indeed.
*Othello*
    By heaven, I'll know thy thoughts.
*Iago*
    You cannot, if my heart were in your hand;
    Nor shall not, whilst 'tis in my custody.      165
*Othello*
    Ha!
*Iago*
      O, beware, my lord, of jealousy;
    It is the green-ey'd monster which doth mock
    The meat it feeds on. That cuckold lives in bliss
    Who, certain of his fate, loves not his wronger;
    But, O, what damned minutes tells he o'er      170
    Who dotes, yet doubts, suspects, yet strongly loves!
*Othello*
    O misery!
*Iago*
    Poor and content is rich, and rich enough;
    But riches fineless is as poor as winter
    To him that ever fears he shall be poor.      175
    Good God, the souls of all my tribe defend
    From jealousy!
*Othello*
          Why, why is this?
    Think'st thou I'd make a life of jealousy,
    To follow still the changes of the moon
    With fresh suspicions? No; to be once in doubt      180

Is once to be resolv'd. Exchange me for a goat
When I shall turn the business of my soul
To such exsufflicate and blown surmises
Matching thy inference. 'Tis not to make me jealous
185 To say my wife is fair, feeds well, loves company,
Is free of speech, sings, plays, and dances well;
Where virtue is, these are more virtuous.
Nor from mine own weak merits will I draw
The smallest fear or doubt of her revolt;
190 For she had eyes, and chose me. No, Iago;
I'll see before I doubt; when I doubt, prove;
And, on the proof, there is no more but this –
Away at once with love or jealousy!

*Iago*

I am glad of this; for now I shall have reason
195 To show the love and duty that I bear you
With franker spirit. Therefore, as I am bound,
Receive it from me. I speak not yet of proof.
Look to your wife; observe her well with Cassio;
Wear your eyes thus, not jealous nor secure.
200 I would not have your free and noble nature
Out of self-bounty be abus'd; look to't.
I know our country disposition well:
In Venice they do let God see the pranks
They dare not show their husbands; their best
conscience
205 Is not to leave't undone, but keep't unknown.

*Othello*

Dost thou say so?

*Iago*

She did deceive her father, marrying you;
And when she seem'd to shake and fear your looks,
She lov'd them most.

*Othello*

And so she did.

*Iago*

Why, go to then!

She that, so young, could give out such a seeming,    210
To seel her father's eyes up close as oak –
He thought 'twas witchcraft. But I am much to blame;
I humbly do beseech you of your pardon
For too much loving you.

*Othello*

               I am bound to thee for ever.

*Iago*

I see this hath a little dash'd your spirits.    215

*Othello*

Not a jot, not a jot.

*Iago*

            I'faith, I fear it has.
I hope you will consider what is spoke
Comes from my love; but I do see you are mov'd.
I am to pray you not to strain my speech
To grosser issues nor to larger reach    220
Than to suspicion.

*Othello*

I will not.

*Iago*

         Should you do so, my lord,
My speech should fall into such vile success
Which my thoughts aim'd not. Cassio's my worthy
   friend –
My lord, I see you are mov'd.

*Othello*

              No, not much mov'd.    225
I do not think but Desdemona's honest.

*Iago*

Long live she so! and long live you to think so!

*Othello*

And yet, how nature erring from itself –

*Iago*

Ay, there's the point: as – to be bold with you –
Not to affect many proposed matches    230
Of her own clime, complexion, and degree,

Whereto we see in all things nature tends –
Foh! one may smell in such a will most rank,
Foul disproportion, thoughts unnatural.
235 But pardon me – I do not in position
Distinctly speak of her; though I may fear
Her will, recoiling to her better judgment,
May fall to match you with her country forms,
And happily repent.

*Othello*

                Farewell, farewell.
240 If more thou dost perceive, let me know more;
Set on thy wife to observe. Leave me, Iago.

*Iago*

My lord, I take my leave. *[Going.]*

*Othello*

Why did I marry? This honest creature doubtless
Sees and knows more – much more than he unfolds.

*Iago*

*[Returning]* My lord, I would I might entreat your
245     honour
To scan this thing no further; leave it to time.
Although 'tis fit that Cassio have his place,
For, sure, he fills it up with great ability,
Yet if you please to hold him off awhile,
250 You shall by that perceive him and his means.
Note if your lady strain his entertainment
With any strong or vehement importunity;
Much will be seen in that. In the mean time
Let me be thought too busy in my fears –
255 As worthy cause I have to fear I am –
And hold her free, I do beseech your honour.

*Othello*

Fear not my government.

*Iago*

I once more take my leave. *[Exit.]*

*Othello*

This fellow's of exceeding honesty,

And knows all qualities, with a learned spirit,       260
Of human dealing. If I do prove her haggard,
Though that her jesses were my dear heart-strings,
I'd whistle her off and let her down the wind
To prey at fortune. Haply, for I am black
And have not those soft parts of conversation       265
That chamberers have, or for I am declin'd
Into the vale of years – yet that's not much –
She's gone; I am abus'd; and my relief
Must be to loathe her. O curse of marriage,
That we can call these delicate creatures ours,       270
And not their appetites! I had rather be a toad,
And live upon the vapour of a dungeon,
Than keep a corner in the thing I love
For others' uses. Yet 'tis the plague of great ones;
Prerogativ'd are they less than the base;       275
'Tis destiny unshunnable, like death:
Even then this forked plague is fated to us
When we do quicken. Look where she comes.

*[Re-enter DESDEMONA and EMILIA.]*

If she be false, O, then heaven mocks itself!
I'll not believe it.
*Desdemona*

          How now, my dear Othello?       280
Your dinner, and the generous islanders
By you invited, do attend your presence.
*Othello*
I am to blame.
*Desdemona*

          Why do you speak so faintly?
Are you not well?
*Othello*
I have a pain upon my forehead here.       285
*Desdemona*
Faith, that's with watching; 'twill away again.
Let me but bind it hard, within this hour

It will be well.

*[He puts the handkerchief from him, and she drops it.]*

*Othello*

       Your napkin is too little.
Let it alone. Come, I'll go in with you.

*Desdemona*

290 I am very sorry that you are not well.

*[Exeunt* OTHELLO *and* DESDEMONA.*]*

*Emilia*

I am glad I have found this napkin.
This was her first remembrance from the Moor.
My wayward husband hath a hundred times
Woo'd me to steal it; but she so loves the token –

295 For he conjur'd her she should ever keep it –
That she reserves it evermore about her
To kiss and talk to. I'll ha the work ta'en out,
And give't Iago. What he'll do with it
Heaven knows, not I;

300 I nothing but to please his fantasy.

*[Re-enter* IAGO.*]*

*Iago*

How now! What do you here alone?

*Emilia*

Do not you chide; I have a thing for you,

*Iago*

You have a thing for me?
It is a common thing!

*Emilia*

305 Ha!

*Iago*

To have a foolish wife.

*Emilia*

O, is that all? What will you give me now
For that same handkerchief?

*Iago*

What handkerchief?

*Emilia*

What handkerchief!
Why that the Moor first gave to Desdemona;          310
That which so often you did bid me steal.

*Iago*

Hast stole it from her?

*Emilia*

No, faith; she let it drop by negligence,
And to the advantage, I, being here, took't up.
Look, here it is.

*Iago*

A good wench! Give it me.          315

*Emilia*

What will you do with't, that you have been so
    earnest
To have me filch it?

*Iago*

Why, what's that to you?

*[Snatching it.]*

*Emilia*

If it be not for some purpose of import,
Give me't again. Poor lady, she'll run mad
When she shall lack it.          320

*Iago*

Be not acknown on't; I have use for it.
Go, leave me.

*[Exit EMILIA.]*

I will in Cassio's lodging lose this napkin,
And let him find it. Trifles light as air
Are to the jealous confirmations strong          325
As proofs of holy writ; this may do something.
The Moor already changes with my poison.
Dangerous conceits are in their natures poisons

Which at the first are scarce found to distaste
330 But, with a little act upon the blood,
Burn like the mines of sulphur.

*[Re-enter OTHELLO.]*

       I did say so.
Look where he comes! Not poppy, nor mandragora,
Nor all the drowsy syrups of the world,
Shall ever medicine thee to that sweet sleep
335 Which thou owed'st yesterday.

*Othello*

Ha! ha! false to me, to me?

*Iago*

Why, how now, General? No more of that.

*Othello*

Avaunt! be gone! Thou hast set me on the rack.
I swear 'tis better to be much abus'd
Than but to know 't a little.

*Iago*

340        How now, my lord!

*Othello*

What sense had I in her stol'n hours of lust?
I saw 't not, thought it not, it harm'd not me.
I slept the next night well, fed well, was free and
  merry;
I found not Cassio's kisses on her lips.
345 He that is robb'd, not wanting what is stol'n,
Let him not know't, and he's not robb'd at all.

*Iago*

I am sorry to hear this.

*Othello*

I had been happy if the general camp,
Pioneers and all, had tasted her sweet body,
350 So I had nothing known. O, now for ever
Farewell the tranquil mind! farewell content!
Farewell the plumed troops, and the big wars
That makes ambition virtue! O, farewell!

Farewell the neighing steed and the shrill trump,
The spirit-stirring drum, th' ear-piercing fife,                    355
The royal banner, and all quality,
Pride, pomp, and circumstance, of glorious war!
And O ye mortal engines whose rude throats
Th' immortal Jove's dread clamours counterfeit,
Farewell! Othello's occupation's gone.                             360

*Iago*
  Is't possible, my lord?
*Othello*
  Villain, be sure thou prove my love a whore –
    *[Taking him by the throat.]*
  Be sure of it; give me the ocular proof;
  Or, by the worth of man's eternal soul,
  Thou hadst been better have been born a dog                      365
  Than answer my wak'd wrath.
*Iago*
                                    Is't come to this?
*Othello*
  Make me to see't; or, at the least, so prove it
  That the probation bear no hinge nor loop
  To hang a doubt on; or woe upon thy life!
*Iago*
  My noble lord –                                                  370
*Othello*
  If thou dost slander her and torture me,
  Never pray more; abandon all remorse;
  On horror's head horrors accumulate;
  Do deeds to make heaven weep, all earth amaz'd;
  For nothing canst thou to damnation add                         375
  Greater than that.
*Iago*
                    O grace! O heaven forgive me!
  Are you a man? Have you a soul or sense? –
  God buy you; take mine office. O wretched fool,
  That liv'st to make thine honesty a vice!
  O monstrous world! Take note, take note, O world,               380

To be direct and honest is not safe.
I thank you for this profit; and from hence
I'll love no friend, sith love breeds such offence.

Othello

Nay, stay. Thou shouldst be honest.

Iago

385 I should be wise; for honesty's a fool,
And loses that it works for.

Othello

By the world,
I think my wife be honest, and think she is not;
I think that thou art just, and think thou art not.
I'll have some proof. Her name, that was as fresh
390 As Dian's visage, is now begrim'd and black
As mine own face. If there be cords or knives,
Poison, or fire, or suffocating streams,
I'll not endure it. Would I were satisfied!

Iago

I see, sir, you are eaten up with passion;
395 I do repent me that I put it to you.
You would be satisfied?

Othello

Would! Nay, and I will.

Iago

And may; but how – how satisfied, my lord?
Would you, the supervisor, grossly gape on –
Behold her topp'd?

Othello

Death and damnation! O!

Iago

400 It were a tedious difficulty, I think,
To bring them to that prospect. Damn them, then,
If ever mortal eyes do see them bolster
More than their own! What then? How then?
What shall I say? Where's satisfaction?
405 It is impossible you should see this,
Were they as prime as goats, as hot as monkeys,

As salt as wolves in pride, and fools as gross
As ignorance made drunk. But yet, I say,
If imputation and strong circumstances
Which lead directly to the door of truth                    410
Will give you satisfaction, you might have't.

*Othello*

Give me a living reason she's disloyal.

*Iago*

I do not like the office;
But, sith I am enter'd in this cause so far,
Prick'd to't by foolish honesty and love,                   415
I will go on. I lay with Cassio lately,
And, being troubled with a raging tooth,
I could not sleep.
There are a kind of men so loose of soul
That in their sleeps will mutter their affairs:             420
One of this kind is Cassio.
In sleep I heard him say 'Sweet Desdemona,
Let us be wary, let us hide our loves',
And then, sir, would he gripe and wring my hand,
Cry 'O sweet creature!' then kiss me hard,                  425
As if he pluck'd up kisses by the roots,
That grew upon my lips – then laid his leg
Over my thigh – and sigh'd, and kiss'd, and then
Cried 'Cursed fate that gave thee to the Moor!'

*Othello*

O Monstrous! Monstrous!                                     430

*Iago*

Nay, this was but his dream.

*Othello*

But this denoted a foregone conclusion.

*Iago*

'Tis a shrewd doubt, though it be but a dream,
And this may help to thicken other proofs
That do demonstrate thinly.                                 435

*Othello*

I'll tear her all to pieces.

*Iago*

    Nay, but be wise; yet we see nothing done;
    She may be honest yet. Tell me but this:
    Have you not sometimes seen a handkerchief
440    Spotted with strawberries in your wife's hand?

*Othello*

    I gave her such a one; 'twas my first gift.

*Iago*

    I know not that; but such a handkerchief –
    I am sure it was your wife's – did I to-day
    See Cassio wipe his beard with.

*Othello*

                    If it be that –

*Iago*

445    If it be that, or any that was hers,
    It speaks against her with the other proofs.

*Othello*

    O that the slave had forty thousand lives!
    One is too poor, too weak for my revenge.
    Now do I see 'tis true. Look here, Iago –
450    All my fond love thus do I blow to heaven.
    'Tis gone.
    Arise, black vengeance, from the hollow hell.
    Yield up, O love, thy crown and hearted throne
    To tyrannous hate! Swell, bosom, with thy fraught,
    For 'tis of aspics' tongues.

*Iago*

455                    Yet Be Content.

*Othello*

    O, blood, blood, blood!

*Iago*

    Patience, I say; your mind perhaps may change.

*Othello*

    Never, Iago. Like to the Pontic sea,
    Whose icy current and compulsive course
460    Ne'er feels retiring ebb, but keeps due on
    To the Propontic and the Hellespont;

Even so my bloody thoughts, with violent pace,
Shall ne'er look back, ne'er ebb to humble love,
Till that a capable and wide revenge
Swallow them up. *[He kneels]* Now, by yond marble
    heaven,                               465
In the due reverence of a sacred vow
I here engage my words.

*Iago*

                    *[Kneeling]* Do not rise yet.
Witness, you ever-burning lights above,
You elements that clip us round about,
Witness that here Iago doth give up          470
The execution of his wit, hands, heart,
To wrong'd Othello's service! Let him command,
And to obey shall be in me remorse,
What bloody business ever. *[They rise.]*

*Othello*

                    I greet thy love,
Not with vain thanks, but with acceptance
    bounteous,                              475
And will upon the instant put thee to't.
Within these three days let me hear thee say
That Cassio's not alive.

*Iago*

                My friend is dead;
'Tis done at your request. But let her live.

*Othello*

Damn her, lewd minx! O, damn her, damn her!   480
Come, go with me apart; I will withdraw
To furnish me with some swift means of death
For the fair devil. Now art thou my lieutenant.

*Iago*

I am your own for ever. *[Exeunt.]*

# SCENE IV

*Cyprus. Before the citadel.*

*[Enter DESDEMONA, EMILIA, and Clown.]*

**Desdemona**

Do you know, sirrah, where the Lieutenant Cassio lies?

**Clown**

I dare not say he lies anywhere.

**Desdemona**

Why, man?

**Clown**

5 He's a soldier; and for one to say a soldier lies, 'tis stabbing.

**Desdemona**

Go to. Where lodges he?

**Clown**

To tell you where he lodges is to tell you where I lie.

**Desdemona**

Can anything be made of this?

**Clown**

I know not where he lodges; and for me to devise a
10 lodging, and say he lies here or he lies there, were to lie in mine own throat.

**Desdemona**

Can you inquire him out, and be edified by report?

**Clown**

I will catechize the world for him; that is, make questions, and by them answer.

**Desdemona**

15 Seek him; bid him come hither: tell him I have mov'd my lord on his behalf, and hope all will be well.

**Clown**

To do this is within the compass of man's wit; and therefore I will attempt the doing it. *[Exit.]*

*Desdemona*
Where should I lose the handkerchief, Emilia?
*Emilia*
I know not, madam.                                    20
*Desdemona*
Believe me, I had rather lose my purse
Full of crusadoes; and but my noble Moor
Is true of mind, and made of no such baseness
As jealous creatures are, it were enough
To put him to ill thinking.
*Emilia*
                              Is he not jealous?       25
*Desdemona*
Who, he? I think the sun where he was born
Drew all such humours from him.

*[Enter OTHELLO.]*

*Emilia*
                                  Look where he comes.
*Desdemona*
I will not leave him now till Cassio
Be call'd to him. How is't with you, my lord?
*Othello*
Well, my good lady. *[Aside]* O,
     hardness to dissemble! –                          30
How do you, Desdemona?
*Desdemona*
                              Well, my good lord.
*Othello*
Give me your hand. This hand is moist, my lady.
*Desdemona*
It yet hath felt no age nor known no sorrow.
*Othello*
This argues fruitfulness and liberal heart:
Hot, hot, and moist. This hand of yours requires     35
A sequester from liberty, fasting and prayer,
Much castigation, exercise devout;

For here's a young and sweating devil here
That commonly rebels. 'Tis a good hand,
40    A frank one.
*Desdemona*
You may indeed say so;
For 'twas that hand that gave away my heart.
*Othello*
A liberal hand. The hearts of old gave hands;
But our new heraldry is hands, not hearts.
*Desdemona*
45    I cannot speak of this. Come now, your promise.
*Othello*
What promise, chuck?
*Desdemona*
I have sent to bid Cassio come speak with you.
*Othello*
I have a salt and sorry rheum offends me;
Lend me thy handkerchief.
*Desdemona*

Here, my lord.
*Othello*
That which I gave you.
*Desdemona*
50                            I have it not about me.
*Othello*
Not?
*Desdemona*
No, faith, my lord.
*Othello*
That's a fault. That handkerchief
Did an Egyptian to my mother give.
She was a charmer, and could almost read
The thoughts of people; she told her, while she kept
55    it,
'Twould make her amiable, and subdue my father
Entirely to her love; but if she lost it,
Or made a gift of it, my father's eye

Should hold her loathely, and his spirits should
　　hunt
After new fancies. She, dying, gave it me,　　　　　60
And bid me, when my fate would have me wive,
To give it her. I did so; and take heed on't;
Make it a darling like your precious eye;
To lose't or give't away were such perdition
As nothing else could match.

*Desdemona*

　　　　　　　　　　Is't possible?　　　　　65

*Othello*

'Tis true. There's magic in the web of it.
A sibyl that had numb'red in the world
The sun to course two hundred compasses
In her prophetic fury sew'd the work;
The worms were hallowed that did breed the silk;　　70
And it was dy'd in mummy which the skilful
Conserv'd of maidens' hearts.

*Desdemona*

　　　　　　　　　　I'faith! Is't true?

*Othello*

Most veritable; therefore look to't well.

*Desdemona*

Then would to God that I had never seen't!

*Othello*

Ha! Wherefore?　　　　　　　　　　75

*Desdemona*

Why do you speak so startingly and rash?

*Othello*

Is't lost? Is't gone? Speak. Is 't out o' th' way?

*Desdemona*

Heaven bless us!

*Othello*

Say you?

*Desdemona*

It is not lost; but what an if it were?　　　　　80

*Othello*
How!

*Desdemona*
I say it is not lost.

*Othello*
            Fetch't, let me see't.

*Desdemona*
Why, so I can, sir, but I will not now.
This is a trick to put me from my suit:

85   Pray you let Cassio be receiv'd again.

*Othello*
Fetch me the handkerchief: my mind misgives.

*Desdemona*
Come, come;
You'll never meet a more sufficient man.

*Othello*
The handkerchief!

*Desdemona*
          I pray talk me of Cassio.

*Othello*
The handkerchief!

*Desdemona*
90          A man that all his time
Hath founded his good fortunes on your love,
Shar'd dangers with you –

*Othello*
            The handkerchief!

*Desdemona*
I'faith, you are to blame.

*Othello*
Zounds! *[Exit OTHELLO.]*

*Emilia*
95   Is not this man jealous?

*Desdemona*
I ne'er saw this before.
Sure there's some wonder in this handkerchief;
I am most unhappy in the loss of it.

*Emilia*

    'Tis not a year or two shows us a man.

    They are all but stomachs, and we all but food;    100

    They eat us hungerly, and when they are full,

    They belch us.

        *[Enter* CASSIO *and* IAGO.*]*

        Look you, Cassio and my husband.

*Iago*

    There is no other way; 'tis she must do 't.

    And, lo, the happiness! Go and importune her.

*Desdemona*

    How now, good Cassio, what's the news with you?    105

*Cassio*

    Madam, my former suit. I do beseech you

    That by your virtuous means I may again

    Exist, and be a member of his love

    Whom I, with all the office of my heart,

    Entirely honour. I would not be delay'd.    110

    If my offence be of such mortal kind

    That nor my service past, nor present sorrows,

    Nor purpos'd merit in futurity,

    Can ransom me into his love again,

    But to know so must be my benefit;    115

    So shall I clothe me in a forc'd content,

    And shut myself up in some other course,

    To fortune's alms.

*Desdemona*

        Alas, thrice-gentle Cassio!

    My advocation is not now in tune;

    My lord is not my lord; nor should I know him,    120

    Were he in favour as in humour alter'd.

    So help me every spirit sanctified,

    As I have spoken for you all my best,

    And stood within the blank of his displeasure

    For my free speech! You must awhile be patient.    125

    What I can do I will; and more I will

    Than for myself I dare; let that suffice you.

*Iago*

Is my lord angry?

*Emilia*

He went hence but now,
And certainly in strange unquietness.

*Iago*

130  Can he be angry? I have seen the cannon
When it hath blown his ranks into the air,
And, like the devil, from his very arm
Puff'd his own brother – and is he angry?
Something of moment, then. I will go meet him.

135  There's matter in't indeed, if he be angry.

*Desdemona*

I prithee do so. *[Exit* IAGO.*]*
Something sure of state
Either from Venice, or some unhatch'd practice
Made demonstrable here in Cyprus to him,
Hath puddled his clear spirit; and in such cases

140  Men's natures wrangle with inferior things,
Though great ones are their object. 'Tis even so;
For let our finger ache, and it endues
Our other healthful members even to a sense
Of pain. Nay, we must think, men are not gods,

145  Nor of them look for such observancy
As fits the bridal. Beshrew me much, Emilia,
I was – unhandsome warrior as I am –
Arraigning his unkindness with my soul;
But now I find I had suborn'd the witness,

150  And he's indicted falsely.

*Emilia*

Pray heaven it be state matters, as you think,
And no conception nor no jealous toy
Concerning you.

*Desdemona*

Alas the day, I never gave him cause!

*Emilia*

155  But jealous souls will not be answer'd so;
They are not ever jealous for the cause,

But jealous for they are jealous. 'Tis a monster
Begot upon it self, born on it self.

Desdemona

Heaven keep that monster from Othello's mind!

Emilia

Lady, amen.                                              160

Desdemona

I will go seek him. Cassio, walk hereabout.
If I do find him fit, I'll move your suit,
And seek to effect it to my uttermost.

Cassio

I humbly thank your ladyship.

*[Exeunt DESDEMONA and EMILIA.]*

*[Enter BIANCA.]*

Bianca

Save you, friend Cassio!

Cassio

                          What make you from home?  165
How is it with you, my most fair Bianca?
I' faith, sweet love, I was coming to your house.

Bianca

And I was going to your lodging, Cassio.
What, keep a week away? seven days and nights?
Eightscore eight hours? and lovers' absent hours,    170
More tedious than the dial eight score times?
O weary reckoning!

Cassio

                    Pardon me, Bianca.
I have this while with leaden thoughts been press'd;
But I shall in a more continuate time
Strike off this score of absence. Sweet Bianca,     175

*[Giving her DESDEMONA's handkerchief.]*

Take me this work out.

*Bianca*

O Cassio, whence came this?
This is some token from a newer friend:
To the felt absence now I feel a cause.
Is't come to this? Well, well.

*Cassio*

Go to, woman!
180    Throw your vile guesses in the devil's teeth,
From whence you have them. You are jealous now
That this is from some mistress, some remembrance.
No, by my faith, Bianca.

*Bianca*

Why, whose is it?

*Cassio*

I know not neither; I found it in my chamber.
185    I like the work well; ere it be demanded –
As like enough it will – I would have it copied.
Take it, and do't; and leave me for this time.

*Bianca*

Leave you! Wherefore?

*Cassio*

I do attend here on the General;
190    And think it no addition, nor my wish,
To have him see me woman'd.

*Bianca*

Why, I pray you?

*Cassio*

Not that I love you not.

*Bianca*

But that you do not love me.
I pray you bring me on the way a little;
And say if I shall see you soon at night.

*Cassio*

195    'Tis but a little way that I can bring you,
For I attend here; but I'll see you soon.

*Bianca*

'Tis very good; I must be circumstanc'd.

*[Exeunt.]*

# ACT FOUR
## SCENE I

*Cyprus. Before the citadel.*

*[Enter* OTHELLO *and* IAGO.*]*

*Iago*
　Will you think so?
*Othello*
　　　　　　　Think so, Iago?
*Iago*
　　　　　　　　　　　What,
　To kiss in private?
*Othello*
　　　　　　　　An unauthoriz'd kiss.
*Iago*
　Or to be naked with her friend abed
　An hour or more, not meaning any harm?
*Othello*
　Naked abed, Iago, and not mean harm!　　　　5
　It is hypocrisy against the devil.
　They that mean virtuously and yet do so,
　The devil their virtue tempts, and they tempt
　　　heaven.
*Iago*
　So they do nothing, 'tis a venial slip;
　But if I give my wife a handkerchief –　　　　10
*Othello*
　What then?
*Iago*
　Why, then 'tis hers, my lord; and, being hers,
　She may, I think, bestow't on any man.
*Othello*
　She is protectress of her honour too:
　May she give that?　　　　　　　　　　　15

*Iago*

Her honour is an essence that's not seen;
They have it very oft that have it not.
But, for the handkerchief –

*Othello*

By heaven, I would most gladly have forgot it.
20   Thou said'st – O, it comes o'er my memory
As doth the raven o'er the infected house,
Boding to all – he had my handkerchief.

*Iago*

Ay, what of that?

*Othello*

That's not so good now.

*Iago*

What
If I had said I had seen him do you wrong?
25   Or heard him say – as knaves be such abroad,
Who having, by their own importunate suit,
Or voluntary dotage of some mistress,
Convinced or supplied them, cannot choose
But they must blab –

*Othello*

Hath he said anything?

*Iago*

30   He hath, my lord; but be you well assur'd,
No more than he'll unswear.

*Othello*

What hath he said?

*Iago*

Faith, that he did – I know not what he did.

*Othello*

What? what?

*Iago*

Lie –

*Othello*

With her?

*Iago*

              With her, on her; what you will.    35

*Othello*

Lie with her – lie on her? We say lie on her when they
belie her. Lie with her. Zounds, that's fulsome.
Handkerchief – confessions – handkerchief! To confess,
and be hang'd for his labour – first, to be hang'd, and
then to confess. I tremble at it. Nature would not invest 40
herself in such shadowing passion without some
instruction. It is not words that shakes me thus – pish!
– noses, ears, and lips. Is't possible? Confess!
Handkerchief! O devil!

*[Falls in a trance.]*

*Iago*

Work on,    45
My medicine, work. Thus credulous fools are caught;
And many worthy and chaste dames even thus,
All guiltless, meet reproach. What, ho! my lord!
My lord, I say! Othello!

*[Enter CASSIO.]*

How now, Cassio!    50

*Cassio*

What's the matter?

*Iago*

My lord is fall'n into an epilepsy.
This is his second fit; he had one yesterday.

*Cassio*

Rub him about the temples.

*Iago*

              No, forbear.
The lethargy must have his quiet course;    55
If not, he foams at mouth, and by and by
Breaks out to savage madness. Look, he stirs.
Do you withdraw yourself a little while;
He will recover straight; when he is gone,

60    I would on great occasion speak with you.

*[Exit CASSIO.]*

How is it, General? Have you not hurt your head?
**Othello**
Dost thou mock me?
**Iago**
                I mock you? No, by heaven!
Would you would bear your fortune like a man!
**Othello**
A horned man's a monster and a beast.
**Iago**
65    There's many a beast then in a populous city,
And many a civil monster.
**Othello**
Did he confess it?
**Iago**
                Good sir, be a man;
Think every bearded fellow that's but yok'd
May draw with you; there's millions now alive
70    That nightly lie in those unproper beds
Which they dare swear peculiar: your case is better.
O, 'tis the spite of hell, the fiend's arch-mock,
To lip a wanton in a secure couch,
And to suppose her chaste! No, let me know;
75    And knowing what I am, I know what she shall be.
**Othello**
O, thou art wise; 'tis certain.
**Iago**
    Stand you awhile apart.
Confine yourself but in a patient list.
Whilst you were here o'erwhelmed with your grief –
80    A passion most unsuiting such a man –
Cassio came hither; I shifted him away,
And laid good 'scuse upon your ecstasy;
Bade him anon return, and here speak with me;
The which he promis'd. Do but encave yourself,
85    And mark the fleers, the gibes, and notable scorns,

That dwell in every region of his face;
For I will make him tell the tale anew –
Where, how, how oft, how long ago, and when,
He hath, and is again to cope your wife.
I say, but mark his gesture. Marry, patience;                90
Or I shall say you are all in all in spleen,
And nothing of a man.

**Othello**

           Dost thou hear, Iago?
I will be found most cunning in my patience;
But – dost thou hear? – most bloody.

**Iago**

                That's not amiss;
But yet keep time in all. Will you withdraw?              95

*[OTHELLO withdraws.]*

Now will I question Cassio of Bianca,
A huswife that by selling her desires
Buys herself bread and clothes; it is a creature
That dotes on Cassio, as 'tis the strumpet's plague
To beguile many and be beguil'd by one.                   100
He, when he hears of her, cannot restrain
From the excess of laughter.

*[Re-enter CASSIO.]*

           Here he comes.
As he shall smile Othello shall go mad;
And his unbookish jealousy must construe
Poor Cassio's smiles, gestures, and light behaviours,     105
Quite in the wrong. How do you now, Lieutenant?

**Cassio**

The worser that you give me the addition Whose want
even kills me.

**Iago**

Ply Desdemona well, and you are sure on't.
Now, if this suit lay in Bianca's dower,                  110
How quickly should you speed!

*Cassio*

Alas, poor caitiff!

*Othello*

Look how he laughs already!

*Iago*

I never knew a woman love man so.

*Cassio*

Alas, poor rogue! I think, i' faith, she loves me.

*Othello*

115  Now he denies it faintly, and laughs it out.

*Iago*

Do you hear, Cassio?

*Othello*

Now he importunes him
To tell it o'er. Go to; well said, well said.

*Iago*

She gives it out that you shall marry her.
Do you intend it?

*Cassio*

120  Ha, ha, ha!

*Othello*

Do you triumph, Roman? Do you triumph?

*Cassio*

I marry her! What, a customer! I prithee bear some
charity to my wit; do not think it so unwholesome.
Ha, ha, ha!

*Othello*

125  So, so, so, so – they laugh that wins.

*Iago*

Faith, the cry goes that you marry her.

*Cassio*

Prithee say true.

*Iago*

I am a very villain else.

*Othello*

Ha you scor'd me? Well.

*Cassio*

This is the monkey's own giving out: she is persuaded 130
I will marry her, out of her own love and flattery, not
out of my promise.

*Othello*

Iago beckons me; now he begins the story.

*Cassio*

She was here even now; she haunts me in every place.
I was t'other day talking on the sea-bank with certain 135
Venetians, and thither comes the bauble – by this
hand, she falls me thus about my neck.

*Othello*

Crying 'O dear Cassio!' as it were: his gesture imports
it.

*Cassio*

So hangs, and lolls, and weeps upon me; so hales, and 140
pulls me. Ha, ha, ha!

*Othello*

Now he tells how she pluck'd him to my chamber.
O, I see that nose of yours, but not that dog I shall
throw't to.

*Cassio*

Well, I must leave her company. 145

*[Enter* BIANCA.*]*

*Iago*

Before me! Look where she comes.

*Cassio*

'Tis such another fitchew! marry, a perfum'd one. What
do you mean by this haunting of me?

*Bianca*

Let the devil and his dam haunt you. What did you
mean by that same handkerchief you gave me even 150
now? I was a fine fool to take it. I must take out the
whole work – a likely piece of work that you should
find it in your chamber and know not who left it there!
This is some minx's token, and I must take out the

155 work? There – give it your hobby-horse. Wheresoever
you had it, I'll take out no work on't.

**Cassio**

How now, my sweet Bianca! how now! how now!

**Othello**

By heaven, that should be my handkerchief!

**Bianca**

An you'll come to supper to-night, you may; an you

160 will not, come when you are next prepar'd for. *[Exit.]*

**Iago**

After her, after her.

**Cassio**

Faith, I must; she'll rail i' th' street else.

**Iago**

Will you sup there?

**Cassio**

Faith, I intend so.

**Iago**

165 Well, I may chance to see you; for I would very fain
speak with you.

**Cassio**

Prithee come; will you?

**Iago**

Go to; say no more. *[Exit CASSIO.]*

**Othello**

*[Coming forward]* How shall I murder him, Iago?

**Iago**

170 Did you perceive how he laugh'd at his vice?

**Othello**

O Iago!

**Iago**

And did you see the handkerchief?

**Othello**

Was that mine?

**Iago**

Yours, by this hand. And to see how he prizes the

175 foolish woman your wife! She gave it him, and he hath
giv'n it his whore.

**Othello**

    I would have him nine years a-killing.

    A fine woman! a fair woman! a sweet woman!

**Iago**

    Nay, you must forget that.

**Othello**

    Ay, let her rot, and perish, and be damn'd to-night;  180
    for she shall not live. No, my heart is turn'd to stone;
    I strike it, and it hurts my hand. O, the world hath
    not a sweeter creature; she might lie by an emperor's
    side and command him tasks.

**Iago**

    Nay, that's not your way.  185

**Othello**

    Hang her! I do but say what she is: so delicate with
    her needle, an admirable musician – O, she will sing
    the savageness out of a bear! – of so high and plenteous
    wit and invention.

**Iago**

    She's the worse for all this.  190

**Othello**

    O, a thousand, a thousand times – and then of so
    gentle a condition.

**Iago**

    Ay, too gentle.

**Othello**

    Nay, that's certain. But yet the pity of it, Iago! O, Iago,
    the pity of it, Iago!  195

**Iago**

    If you be so fond over her iniquity, give her patent to
    offend; for, if it touch not you, it comes near nobody.

**Othello**

    I will chop her into messes. Cuckold me!

**Iago**

    O, 'tis foul in her.

*Othello*

200   With mine officer!

*Iago*

    That's fouler.

*Othello*

    Get me some poison, Iago – this night.
    I'll not expostulate with her, lest her body and beauty
    unprovide my mind again – this night, Iago.

*Iago*

205   Do it not with poison; strangle her in her bed, even
    the bed she hath contaminated.

*Othello*

    Good, good; the justice of it pleases; very good.

*Iago*

    And for Cassio – let me be his undertaker.
    You shall hear more by midnight.

*Othello*

    Excellent good. *[A trumpet.]*

210                 What trumpet is that same?

*Iago*

    I warrant, something from Venice.

    *[Enter LODOVICO, DESDEMONA, and Attendants.]*

    'Tis Lodovico – this comes from the Duke.
    See, your wife's with him.

*Lodovico*

    God save thee, worthy General!

*Othello*

                   With all my heart, sir.

*Lodovico*

215   The Duke and Senators of Venice greet you.
    *[Gives him a packet.]*

*Othello*

    I kiss the instrument of their pleasures.

    *[Opens the packet and reads.]*

*Desdemona*

And what's the news, good cousin Lodovico?

*Iago*

I am very glad to see you, signior;
Welcome to Cyprus.

*Lodovico*

I thank you. How does Lieutenant Cassio?                    220

*Iago*

Lives, sir.

*Desdemona*

Cousin, there's fall'n between him and my lord
An unkind breach; but you shall make all well.

*Othello*

Are you sure of that?

*Desdemona*

My lord?                                                    225

*Othello*

[Reads] 'This fail you not to do as you will' –

*Lodovico*

He did not call; he's busy in the paper.
Is there division 'twixt thy lord and Cassio?

*Desdemona*

A most unhappy one. I would do much
T' atone them, for the love I bear to Cassio.               230

*Othello*

Fire and brimstone!

*Desdemona*

My lord?

*Othello*

Are you wise?

*Desdemona*

What, is he angry?

*Lodovico*

                    May be the letter mov'd him;
For, as I think, they do command him home,                  235
Deputing Cassio in his government.

*Desdemona*
By my troth, I am glad on't.
*Othello*
Indeed!
*Desdemona*
My lord?
*Othello*
I am glad to see you mad.
*Desdemona*

240                                            Why, sweet Othello?
*Othello*
Devil! *[Striking her.]*
*Desdemona*
I have not deserv'd this.
*Lodovico*
My lord, this would not be believ'd in Venice,
Though I should swear I saw't. 'Tis very much.
Make her amends; she weeps.
*Othello*

245                                            O devil, devil!
If that the earth could teem with woman's tears,
Each drop she falls would prove a crocodile.
Out of my sight!
*Desdemona*

                    I will not stay to offend you.

*[Going.]*

*Lodovico*
Truly, an obedient lady.
250   I do beseech your lordship, call her back.
*Othello*
Mistress!
*Desdemona*
My lord?
*Othello*
What would you with her, sir?
*Lodovico*

                                    Who, I, my lord?

*Othello*
    Ay; you did wish that I would make her turn.
    Sir, she can turn, and turn, and yet go on,     255
    And turn again; and she can weep, sir, weep;
    And she's obedient, as you say, obedient,
    Very obedient. – Proceed you in your tears. –
    Concerning this, sir, – O, well-painted passion! –
    I am commanded home. – Get you away;     260
    I'll send for you anon. – Sir, I obey the mandate,
    And will return to Venice. – Hence, avaunt!

    *[Exit DESDEMONA.]*

    Cassio shall have my place. And, sir, to-night,
    I do entreat that we may sup together.
    You are welcome, sir, to Cyprus. – Goats and
        monkeys! *[Exit.]*     265
*Lodovico*
    Is this the noble Moor whom our full Senate
    Call all in all sufficient? Is this the nature
    Whom passion could not shake, whose solid virtue
    The shot of accident nor dart of chance
    Could neither graze nor pierce?
*Iago*
                         He is much chang'd.     270
*Lodovico*
    Are his wits safe? Is he not light of brain?
*Iago*
    He's that he is. I may not breathe my censure.
    What he might be, if what he might he is not,
    I would to heaven he were!
*Lodovico*
                         What, strike his wife!
*Iago*
    Faith, that was not so well; yet would I knew     275
    That stroke would prove the worst!
*Lodovico*
                         Is it his use?

Or did the letters work upon his blood,
And new-create this fault?

Iago

Alas, alas!
It is not honesty in me to speak
What I have seen and known. You shall observe
280     him;
And his own courses will denote him so
That I may save my speech. Do but go after,
And mark how he continues.

Lodovico

I am sorry that I am deceiv'd in him.

*[Exeunt.]*

# SCENE II

### Cyprus. The citadel.

*[Enter OTHELLO and EMILIA.]*

*Othello*
You have seen nothing, then?
*Emilia*
Nor ever heard, nor ever did suspect.
*Othello*
Yes, you have seen Cassio and she together.
*Emilia*
But then I saw no harm, and then I heard
Each syllable that breath made up between them.          5
*Othello*
What, did they never whisper?
*Emilia*
Never, my lord.
*Othello*
         Nor send you out o'th' way?
*Emilia*
Never.
*Othello*
To fetch her fan, her gloves, her mask, nor nothing?
*Emilia*
Never, my lord.                                         10
*Othello*
That's strange.
*Emilia*
I durst, my lord, to wager she is honest,
Lay down my soul at stake. If you think other,
Remove your thought – it doth abuse your bosom.
If any wretch have put this in your head,               15
Let heaven requite it with the serpent's curse;
For if she be not honest, chaste, and true,
There's no man happy; the purest of their wives
Is foul as slander.

*Othello*

Bid her come hither. Go.

*[Exit EMILIA.]*

20     She says enough; yet she's a simple bawd
That cannot say as much. This is a subtle whore,
A closet-lock-and-key of villainous secrets;
And yet she'll kneel and pray; I have seen her do't.

*[Re-enter EMILIA with DESDEMONA.]*

*Desdemona*
My lord, what is your will?
*Othello*
25     Pray you chuck, come hither.
*Desdemona*
What is your pleasure?
*Othello*
Let me see your eyes; look in my face.
*Desdemona*
What horrible fancy's this?
*Othello*
*[To EMILIA]* Some of your function, mistress:
30     Leave procreants alone, and shut the door;
Cough, or cry hem, if any body come.
Your mystery, your mystery; nay, dispatch.

*[Exit EMILIA.]*

*Desdemona*
Upon my knees, what doth your speech import?
I understand a fury in your words,
35     But not the words.
*Othello*
Why, what art thou?
*Desdemona*
You wife, my lord; your true and loyal wife.
*Othello*
Come, swear it, damn thyself; lest, being like one of

heaven, the devils themselves should fear to seize thee;
therefore be double-damn'd – swear thou art honest.    40

*Desdemona*

Heaven doth truly know it.

*Othello*

Heaven truly knows that thou art false as hell.

*Desdemona*

To whom, my lord? With whom?
How am I false?

*Othello*

Ah, Desdemona! away! away! away!    45

*Desdemona*

Alas the heavy day! Why do you weep?
Am I the motive of these tears, my lord?
If haply you my father do suspect
An instrument of this your calling back,
Lay not your blame on me; If you have lost him,    50
Why, I have lost him too.

*Othello*

       Had it pleas'd heaven
To try me with affliction; had they rain'd
All kind of sores and shames on my bare head,
Steep'd me in poverty to the very lips,
Given to captivity me and my utmost hopes,    55
I should have found in some place of my soul
A drop of patience; but, alas, to make me
The fixed figure for the time of scorn
To point his slow unmoving finger at! – O, O!
Yet could I bear that too; well, very well;    60
But there, where I have garner'd up my heart,
Where either I must live or bear no life,
The fountain from the which my current runs,
Or else dries up – to be discarded thence!
Or keep it as a cistern for foul toads    65
To knot and gender in! Turn thy complexion there,
Patience, thou young and rose-lipp'd cherubin –
Ay, here, look grim as hell.

*Desdemona*
I hope my noble lord esteems me honest.
*Othello*
70    O, ay; as summer flies are in the shambles,
That quicken even with blowing. O thou weed
Who art so lovely fair and smell'st so sweet
That the sense aches at thee! Would thou had'st never been born!
Would thou had'st never been born!
*Desdemona*
75    Alas, what ignorant sin have I committed?
*Othello*
Was this fair paper, this most goodly book,
Made to write 'whore' upon? What committed!
Committed! O thou public commoner!
I should make very forges of my cheeks
80    That would to cinders burn up modesty,
Did I but speak thy deeds. What committed!
Heaven stops the nose at it, and the moon winks;
The bawdy wind, that kisses all it meets,
Is hush'd within the hollow mine of earth
85    And will not hear it. What committed!
Impudent strumpet!
*Desdemona*
                By heaven, you do me wrong.
*Othello*
Are not you a strumpet?
*Desdemona*
                No, as I am a Christian.
If to preserve this vessel for my lord
From any other foul unlawful touch
90    Be not to be a strumpet, I am none.
*Othello*
What, not a whore?
*Desdemona*
                No, as I shall be sav'd.
*Othello*
Is't possible?

*Desdemona*
> O, heaven forgive us!

*Othello*
>                I cry you mercy, then.
> I took you for that cunning whore of Venice
> That married with Othello. – You, mistress,    95
> That have the office opposite to Saint Peter
> And keeps the gate of hell!

*[Re-enter* EMILIA.*]*

> You, you, ay you!
> We ha done our course; there's money for your
>     pains.
> I pray you turn the key, and keep our counsel.    100

*[Exit.]*

*Emilia*
> Alas, what does this gentleman conceive?
> How do you, madam? How do you, my good lady?

*Desdemona*
> Faith, half asleep.

*Emilia*
> Good madam, what's the matter with my lord?

*Desdemona*
> With who?    105

*Emilia*
> Why, with my lord, madam.

*Desdemona*
> Who is thy lord?

*Emilia*
>                He that is yours, sweet lady.

*Desdemona*
> I have none. Do not talk to me, Emilia;
> I cannot weep, nor answers have I none
> But what should go by water. Prithee, to-night    110
> Lay on my bed my wedding sheets – remember;
> And call thy husband hither.

*Emilia*

Here's a change indeed! *[Exit.]*

*Desdemona*

'Tis meet I should be us'd so, very meet.

115   How have I been behav'd, that he might stick
      The small'st opinion on my great'st abuse?

*[Re-enter EMILIA with IAGO.]*

*Iago*

What is your pleasure, madam? How is't with you?

*Desdemona*

I cannot tell. Those that do teach young babes
Do it with gentle means and easy tasks.

120   He might have child me so; for, in good faith,
      I am a child to chiding.

*Iago*

What is the matter, lady?

*Emilia*

Alas, Iago, my lord hath so bewhor'd her,
Thrown such despite and heavy terms upon her
That true hearts cannot bear it.

*Desdemona*

Am I that name, Iago?

*Iago*

125                           What name, fair lady?

*Desdemona*

Such as she says my lord did say I was.

*Emilia*

He call'd her whore. A beggar in his drink
Could not have laid such terms upon his callat.

*Iago*

Why did he so?

*Desdemona*

130   I do not know; I am sure I am none such.

*Iago*

Do not weep, do not weep. Alas, the day!

*Emilia*

    Hath she forsook so many noble matches,

    Her father, and her country, and her friends,

    To be call'd whore? Would it not make one weep?

*Desdemona*

    It is my wretched fortune.

*Iago*

                       Beshrew him for't!    135

    How comes this trick upon him?

*Desdemona*

                     Nay, heaven doth know.

*Emilia*

    I will be hang'd if some eternal villain,

    Some busy and insinuating rogue,

    Some cogging, cozening slave, to get some office,

    Have not devis'd this slander; I'll be hang'd else.    140

*Iago*

    Fie, there is no such man; it is impossible.

*Desdemona*

    If any such there be, heaven pardon him!

*Emilia*

    A halter pardon him! and hell gnaw his bones!

    Why should he call her whore? Who keeps her

      company?

    What place, what time, what form, what likelihood?  140

    The Moor's abus'd by some outrageous knave,

    Some base notorious knave, some scurvy fellow.

    O heaven, that such companions thou'dst unfold,

    And put in every honest hand a whip

    To lash the rascals naked through the world    150

    Even from the east to the west!

*Iago*

                   Speak within door.

*Emilia*

    O, fie upon them! Some such squire he was

    That turn'd your wit the seamy side without

    And made you to suspect me with the Moor.

*Iago*
    You are a fool; go to.
*Desdemona*
155                 O God! Iago,
    What shall I do to win my lord again?
    Good friend, go to him; for, by this light of heaven,
    I know not how I lost him. Here I kneel.
    If e'er my will did trespass 'gainst his love,
160     Either in discourse of thought or actual deed,
    Or that mine eyes, mine ears, or any sense,
    Delighted them in any other form,
    Or that I do not yet, and ever did,
    And ever will – though he do shake me off
165     To beggarly divorcement – love him dearly,
    Comfort forswear me! Unkindness may do much;
    And his unkindness may defeat my life,
    But never taint my love. I cannot say 'whore';
    It does abhor me now I speak the word;
170     To do the act that might the addition earn,
    Not the world's mass of vanity could make me.
*Iago*
    I pray you be content; 'tis but his humour.
    The business of the state does him offence,
    And he does chide with you.
*Desdemona*
    If 'twere no other!
*Iago*
175               It is but so, I warrant.

*[Trumpets within.]*

    Hark how these instruments summon you to supper.
    The messengers of Venice stay the meat.
    Go in, and weep not; all things shall be well.

*[Exeunt* DESDEMONA *and* EMILIA.*]*

*[Enter* RODERIGO.*]*

How now, Roderigo!

*Roderigo*

I do not find that thou deal'st justly with me.

*Iago*

What in the contrary? 180

*Roderigo*

Every day thou daff'st me with some device, Iago; and rather, as it seems to me now, keep'st from me all conveniency than suppliest me with the least advantage of hope. I will indeed, no longer endure it; nor am I yet persuaded to put up in peace what already I 185 have foolishly suffer'd.

*Iago*

Will you hear me, Roderigo?

*Roderigo*

Faith, I have heard too much; for your words and performances are no kin together.

*Iago*

You charge me most unjustly. 190

*Roderigo*

With nought but truth. I have wasted myself out of my means. The jewels you have had from me to deliver to Desdemona would half have corrupted a votarist. You have told me she hath receiv'd them, and return'd me expectations and comforts of sudden respect and 195 acquaintance; but I find none.

*Iago*

Well; go to; very well.

*Roderigo*

Very well! go to! I cannot go to, man, nor 'tis not very well; by this hand, I say 'tis very scurvy, and begin to find myself fopt in it. 200

*Iago*

Very well.

*Roderigo*

I tell you 'tis not very well. I will make myself known to Desdemona. If she will return me my jewels, I will

give over my suit and repent my unlawful solicitation;
205    if not, assure yourself I will seek satisfaction of you.

*Iago*

You have said now.

*Roderigo*

Ay, and said nothing but what I protest intendment
     of doing.

*Iago*

Why, now I see there's mettle in thee; and even from
this instant do build on thee a better opinion than
210    ever before. Give me thy hand, Roderigo. Thou hast
taken against me a most just exception; but yet, I
protest, I have dealt most directly in thy affair.

*Roderigo*

It hath not appear'd.

*Iago*

I grant, indeed, it hath not appear'd; and your suspicion
215    is not without wit and judgment. But, Roderigo, if thou
hast that in thee indeed, which I have greater reason
to believe now than ever – I mean purpose, courage,
and valour – this night show it; if thou the next night
following enjoy not Desdemona, take me from this
220    world with treachery, and devise engines for my life.

*Roderigo*

Well, what is it? Is it within reason and compass?

*Iago*

Sir, there is especial commission come from Venice to
depute Cassio in Othello's place.

*Roderigo*

Is that true? Why, then Othello and Desdemona return
225    again to Venice.

*Iago*

O, no; he goes into Mauritania, and taketh away with
him the fair Desdemona, unless his abode be linger'd
here by some accident; wherein none can be so deter-
minate as the removing of Cassio.

**Roderigo**

How do you mean removing of him?                    230

**Iago**

Why, by making him uncapable of Othello's place –
knocking out his brains.

**Roderigo**

And that you would have me to do?

**Iago**

Ay, an if you dare do yourself a profit and right. He
sups to-night with a harlotry, and thither will I go to 235
him – he knows not yet of his honourable fortune. If
you will watch his going thence, which I will fashion
to fall out between twelve and one, you may take him
at your pleasure. I will be near to second your attempt,
and he shall fall between us. Come, stand not amaz'd 240
at it, but go along with me; I will show you such a
necessity in his death that you shall think yourself
bound to put it on him. It is now high supper-time,
and the night grows to waste. About it.

**Roderigo**

I will hear further reason for this.                    245

**Iago**

And you shall be satisfied. *[Exeunt.]*

# SCENE III

### *Cyprus. The citadel.*

*[Enter OTHELLO, DESDEMONA, LODOVICO, EMILIA,
and Attendants.]*

*Lodovico*
I do beseech you, sir, trouble yourself no further.
*Othello*
O, pardon me; 'twill do me good to walk.
*Lodovico*
Madam, good night; I humbly thank your ladyship.
*Desdemona*
Your honour is most welcome.
*Othello*
5    Will you walk, sir? O, Desdemona!
*Desdemona*
My lord?
*Othello*
Get you to bed on th' instant; I will be return'd forth-
with. Dispatch your attendant there. Look 't be done.
*Desdemona*
I will, my lord.

*[Exeunt OTHELLO, LODOVICO, and Attendants.]*

*Emilia*
10   How goes it now? He looks gentler than he did.
*Desdemona*
He says he will return incontinent.
He hath commanded me to go to bed,
And bade me to dismiss you.
*Emilia*
                   Dismiss me!
*Desdemona*
It was his bidding; therefore, good Emilia,
15   Give me my nightly wearing, and adieu.
We must not now displease him.

*Emilia*
    I would you had never seen him.
*Desdemona*
    So would not I: my love doth so approve him
    That even his stubbornness, his checks, his frowns –
    Prithee unpin me – have grace and favour in them.    20
*Emilia*
    I have laid those sheets you bade me on the bed.
*Desdemona*
    All's one. Good faith, how foolish are our minds!
    If I do die before thee, prithee shroud me
    In one of these same sheets.
*Emilia*
                                    Come, come, you talk.
*Desdemona*
    My mother had a maid call'd Barbary:                25
    She was in love; and he she lov'd prov'd mad,
    And did forsake her. She had a song of 'willow';
    An old thing 'twas, but it express'd her fortune,
    And she died singing it. That song to-night
    Will not go from my mind; I have much to do        30
    But to go hang my head all at one side
    And sing it like poor Barbary. Prithee dispatch.
*Emilia*
    Shall I go fetch your night-gown?
*Desdemona*
    No, unpin me here.
    This Lodovico is a proper man.                      35
*Emilia*
    A very handsome man.
*Desdemona*
    He speaks well.
*Emilia*
    I know a lady in Venice would have walk'd barefoot
    to Palestine for a touch of his nether lip.
*Desdemona*
    [Sings] The poor soul sat sighing by a sycamore tree,    40

> Sing all a green willow;
> Her hand on her bosom, her head on her knee.
>> Sing willow, willow, willow.
> The fresh streams ran by her, and murmur'd her
>    moans;

45
>>> Sing willow, willow, willow;
> Her salt tears fell from her and soft'ned the stones;
>> Sing willow –
> Lay by these –
>> willow, willow. –
> Prithee, hie thee; he'll come anon. –

50
> Sing all a green willow must be my garland.
> Let nobody blame him; his scorn I approve –
> Nay, that's not next. Hark! who is't that knocks?

*Emilia*

It is the wind.

*Desdemona*

*[Sings]* I call'd my love false love; but what said he
   then?

55
> Sing willow, willow, willow:
> If I court moe women, you'll couch with moe men –
> So, get thee gone; good night. Mine eyes do itch;
> Doth that bode weeping?

*Emilia*

                              'Tis neither here nor there.

*Desdemona*

I have heard it said so. O, these men, these men!

60
Dost thou in conscience think – tell me, Emilia –
That there be women do abuse their husbands
In such gross kind?

*Emilia*

                         There be some such, no question.

*Desdemona*

Wouldst thou do such a deed for all the world?

*Emilia*

Why, would not you?

*Desdemona*

          No, by this heavenly light!

*Emilia*

Nor I neither by this heavenly light;        65
I might do't as well i' th' dark.

*Desdemona*

Wouldst thou do such a deed for all the world?

*Emilia*

The world's a huge thing.
It is a great price for a small vice.

*Desdemona*

Good troth, I think thou wouldst not.       70

*Emilia*

By my troth, I think I should; and undo't when I had
done it. Marry, I would not do such a thing for a
joint-ring, nor for measures of lawn, nor for gowns,
petticoats, nor caps, nor any petty exhibition; but for
all the whole world – ud's pity, who would not make   75
her husband a cuckold to make him a monarch? I
should venture purgatory for't.

*Desdemona*

Beshrew me, if I would do such a wrong for the whole
world.

*Emilia*

Why, the wrong is but a wrong i' th' world; and having   80
the world for your labour, 'tis a wrong in your own
world, and you might quickly make it right.

*Desdemona*

I do not think there is any such woman.

*Emilia*

Yes, a dozen; and as many to th' vantage
as would store the world they play'd for.       85
But I do think it is their husbands' faults
If wives do fall. Say that they slack their duties,
And pour our treasures into foreign laps;
Or else break out in peevish jealousies,
Throwing restraint upon us; or say they strike us,    90

Or scant our former having in despite;
Why, we have galls; and though we have some
    grace,
Yet have we some revenge. Let husbands know
Their wives have sense like them; they see and
    smell,
95    And have their palates both for sweet and sour
As husbands have. What is it that they do
When they change us for others? Is it sport?
I think it is. And doth affection breed it?
I think it doth. Is't frailty that thus errs?
100    It is so too. And have not we affections,
Desires for sport, and frailty, as men have?
Then let them use us well; else let them know
The ills we do their ills instruct us so.

*Desdemona*

Good night, good night. God me such uses send,
105    Not to pick bad from bad, but by bad mend!

*[Exeunt.]*

126

# ACT FIVE

# SCENE I

### *Cyprus. A street.*

*[Enter* IAGO *and* RODERIGO.*]*

*Iago*

Here, stand behind this bulk; straight will he come.
Wear thy good rapier bare, and put it home.
Quick, quick; fear nothing; I'll be at thy elbow.
It makes us or it mars us; think on that,
And fix most firm thy resolution.                    5

*Roderigo*

Be near at hand; I may miscarry in't.

*Iago*

Here, at thy hand. Be bold, and take thy stand.
    *[Withdraws.]*

*Roderigo*

I have no great devotion to the deed;
And yet he hath given me satisfying reasons –
'Tis but a man gone. Forth, my sword; he dies.       10

*Iago*

I have rubb'd this young quat almost to the sense,
And he grows angry. Now, whether he kill Cassio
Or Cassio him, or each do kill the other,
Every way makes my gain. Live Roderigo,
He calls me to a restitution large                   15
Of gold and jewels that I bobb'd from him
As gifts to Desdemona;
It must not be. If Cassio do remain,
He hath a daily beauty in his life
That makes me ugly; and besides, the Moor            20
May unfold me to him; there stand I in much peril.
No, he must die. Be 't so. I hear him coming.

*[Enter* CASSIO.*]*

*Roderigo*
I know his gait, 'tis he. Villain, thou diest!
    *[Thrusts at* CASSIO.*]*

*Cassio*
That thrust had been mine enemy indeed
25  But that my coat is better than thou know'st.
I will make proof of thine. *[Draws, and wounds*
    RODERIGO.*]*

*Roderigo*
O, I am slain! *[*IAGO *stabs Cassio from behind in the*
    *leg, and exit.]*

*Cassio*
I am maim'd for ever. Help, ho! murder! murder!
    *[Falls.]*

        *[Enter* OTHELLO *at a distance.]*

*Othello*
The voice of Cassio. Iago keeps his word.

*Roderigo*
30  O, villain that I am!

*Othello*
It is even so.

*Cassio*
O, help, ho! light! a surgeon!

*Othello*
'Tis he. O brave Iago, honest and just,
That hast such noble sense of thy friend's wrong!
35  Thou teachest me – minion, your dear lies dead,
And your unblest fate hies. Strumpet, I come.
Forth of my heart those charms, thine eyes, are
    blotted;
Thy bed, lust-stain'd, shall with lust's blood be
    spotted. *[Exit.]*

        *[Enter* LODOVICO *and* GRATIANO *at a distance.]*

*Cassio*
What, ho! No watch? No passage?

Murder! murder! 40

*Gratiano*
'Tis some mischance; the voice is very direful.

*Cassio*
O, help!

*Lodovico*
Hark!

*Roderigo*
O wretched villain!

*Lodovico*
Two or three groan. 'Tis heavy night; 45
These may be counterfeits; let's think't unsafe
To come in to the cry without more help.

*Roderigo*
Nobody come? Then shall I bleed to death.

*[Re-enter* IAGO *with a light.]*

*Lodovico*
Hark!

*Gratiano*
Here's one comes in his shirt, with light and weapons. 50

*Iago*
Who's there? Whose noise is this that cries on murder?

*Lodovico*
We do not know.

*Iago*
              Did not you hear a cry?

*Cassio*
Here, here! For heaven's sake, help me!

*Iago*
                    What's the matter?

*Gratiano*
This is Othello's ancient, as I take it.

*Lodovico*
The same indeed; a very valiant fellow. 55

*Iago*
What are you here that cry so grievously?

*Cassio*
    Iago? O, I am spoil'd, undone by villains!
    Give me some help.
*Iago*
    O me, Lieutenant! What villains have done this?
*Cassio*
60   I think that one of them is hereabout,
    And cannot make away.
*Iago*

                       O treacherous villains! –
    *[To* LODOVICO *and* GRATIANO*]*    What are you there?
      Come in, and give some help.
*Roderigo*
    O, help me there!
*Cassio*
    That's one of them.
*Iago*
65   O murd'rous slave! O villian!

                *[Stabs* RODERIGO*.]*

*Roderigo*
    O damn'd Iago! O inhuman dog!
*Iago*
    Kill men i' th' dark! Where be these bloody thieves?
    How silent is this town. Ho! murder! murder!
    What may you be? Are you of good or evil?
*Lodovico*
70   As you shall prove us, praise us.
*Iago*
    Signior Lodovico?
*Lodovico*
    He, sir.
*Iago*
    I cry you mercy. Here's Cassio hurt by villains.
*Gratiano*
    Cassio!

*Iago*

How is't, brother?                                    75

*Cassio*

My leg is cut in two.

*Iago*

Marry, heaven forbid!

Light, gentlemen. I'll bind it with my shirt.

*[Enter* BIANCA.*]*

*Bianca*

What is the matter, ho? Who is't that cried?

*Iago*

Who is't that cried!                                  80

*Bianca*

O my dear Cassio!

My sweet Cassio! O Cassio, Cassio, Cassio!

*Iago*

O notable strumpet! Cassio, may you suspect

Who they should be that have thus mangled you?

*Cassio*

No.                                                   85

*Gratiano*

I am sorry to find you thus; I have been to seek you.

*Iago*

Lend me a garter. So.

O, for a chair, to bear him easily hence!

*Bianca*

Alas, he faints! O Cassio, Cassio, Cassio!

*Iago*

Gentlemen all, I do suspect this trash               90

To be a party in this injury.

Patience awhile, good Cassio. Come, come;

Lend me a light. Know we this face or no?

Alas, my friend and my dear countryman

Roderigo? No – yes, sure; O heaven! Roderigo.        95

*Gratiano*

What, of Venice?

*Iago*
    Even he, sir; did you know him?
*Gratiano*

                                    Know him! Ay.

*Iago*
    Signior Gratiano? I cry your gentle pardon;
    These bloody accidents must excuse my manners,
    That so neglected you.
*Gratiano*
100                                    I am glad to see you.
*Iago*
    How do you, Cassio? – O, a chair, a chair!
*Gratiano*
    Roderigo!
*Iago*
    He, he, 'tis he. *[A chair brought in.]*
    O, that's well said; the chair.
105 Some good man bear him carefully from hence;
    I'll fetch the General's surgeon. *[To* BIANCA*]* For you,
        mistress,
    Save you your labour. – He that lies slain here,
        Cassio,
    Was my dear friend. What malice was between you?
*Cassio*
    None in the world; nor do I know the man.
*Iago*
    *[To* BIANCA*]* What, look you pale? – O, bear him out
110     o' th' air.

              *[CASSIO and RODERIGO are borne off.]*

    Stay you, good gentlemen. – Look you pale,
        mistress? –
    Do you perceive the gastness of her eye? –
    Nay, an you stare, we shall hear more anon. –
    Behold her well; I pray you look upon her.
115 Do you see, gentlemen? Nay, guiltiness will speak
    Though tongues were out of use.

*[Enter EMILIA.]*

*Emilia*
'Las, what's the matter? What's the matter, husband?
*Iago*
Cassio hath here been set on in the dark
By Roderigo and fellows that are 'scap'd.
He's almost slain, and Roderigo quite dead.                    120
*Emilia*
Alas, good gentleman! Alas, good Cassio!
*Iago*
This is the fruits of whoring. Prithee, Emilia,
Go know of Cassio where he supp'd to-night. –
What, do you shake at that?
*Bianca*
He supp'd at my house; but I therefore shake not.    125
*Iago*
O, did he so? I charge you go with me.
*Emilia*
Fie, fie upon thee, strumpet!
*Bianca*
I am no strumpet, but of life as honest
As you that thus abuse me.
*Emilia*
                                  As I! Foh! Fie upon thee!
*Iago*
Kind gentlemen, let's go see poor Cassio dress'd. –    130
Come, mistress, you must tell's another tale.
Emilia, run you to the citadel,
And tell my lord and lady what hath happ'd.
Will you go on afore? *[Aside]* This is the night
That either makes me or fordoes me quite.                    135

*[Exeunt.]*

# SCENE II

### *Cyprus. The citadel.*

*[DESDEMONA in her bed. Enter OTHELLO with a light.]*

*Othello*

    It is the cause, it is the cause, my soul –
    Let me not name it to you, you chaste stars –
    It is the cause. Yet I'll not shed her blood,
    Nor scar that whiter skin of hers than snow,
5    And smooth as monumental alabaster.
    Yet she must die, else she'll betray more men.
    Put out the light, and then put out the light.
    If I quench thee, thou flaming minister,
    I can again thy former light restore,
10    Should I repent me; but once put out thy light,
    Thou cunning'st pattern of excelling nature,
    I know not where is that Promethean heat
    That can thy light relume. When I have pluck'd thy rose,
    I cannot give it vital growth again;
15    It needs must wither. I'll smell thee on the tree.

*[Kissing her.]*

    O balmy breath, that dost almost persuade
    Justice to break her sword! One more, one more.
    Be thus when thou art dead, and I will kill thee,
    And love thee after. One more, and that's the last:
20    So sweet was ne'er so fatal. I must weep,
    But they are cruel tears. This sorrow's heavenly;
    It strikes where it doth love. She wakes.

*Desdemona*

    Who's there? Othello?

*Othello*

    Ay, Desdemona.

*Desdemona*

25    Will you come to bed, my lord?

*Othello*
Have you pray'd to-night, Desdemona?
*Desdemona*
Ay, my lord.
*Othello*
If you bethink yourself of any crime
Unreconcil'd as yet to heaven and grace,
Solicit for it straight.
*Desdemona*
                Alack, my lord,        30
What may you mean by that?
*Othello*
Well, do it, and be brief; I will walk by.
I would not kill thy unprepared spirit;
No, heaven forfend! – I would not kill thy soul.
*Desdemona*
Talk you of killing?
*Othello*
              Ay, I do.
*Desdemona*
                 Then heaven        95
Have mercy on me!
*Othello*
          Amen, with all my heart!
*Desdemona*
If you say so, I hope you will not kill me.
*Othello*
Humh!
*Desdemona*
And yet I fear you; for you're fatal then
When your eyes roll so. Why I should fear I know
    not,                                 40
Since guiltiness I know not; but yet I feel I fear.
*Othello*
Think on thy sins.
*Desdemona*
              They are loves I bear to you.

**Othello**

Ay, and for that thou diest.

**Desdemona**

That death's unnatural that kills for loving.
45 Alas, why gnaw you so your nether lip?
Some bloody passion shakes your very frame.
These are portents; but yet I hope, I hope,
They do not point on me.

**Othello**

Peace, and be still.

**Desdemona**

I will so. What's the matter?

**Othello**

50 That handkerchief which I so lov'd and gave thee
Thou gav'st to Cassio.

**Desdemona**

No, by my life and soul!
Send for the man and ask him.

**Othello**

Sweet soul, take heed,
Take heed of perjury; thou art on thy death-bed.

**Desdemona**

Ay, but not yet to die.

**Othello**

Yes, presently.
55 Therefore confess thee freely of thy sin;
For to deny each article with oath
Cannot remove nor choke the strong conception
That I do groan withal. Thou art to die.

**Desdemona**

Then, Lord have mercy on me!

**Othello**

I say, amen.

**Desdemona**

60 And have you mercy too! I never did
Offend you in my life; never lov'd Cassio
But with such general warranty of heaven

As I might love. I never gave him token.

**Othello**
By heaven, I saw my handkerchief in's hand.
O perjur'd woman! thou dost stone my heart,                    65
And mak'st me call what I intend to do
A murder, which I thought a sacrifice.
I saw the handkerchief.

**Desdemona**
              He found it, then;
I never gave it him. Send for him hither;
Let him confess a truth.

**Othello**
              He hath confess'd.          70

**Desdemona**
What, my lord?

**Othello**
That he hath – ud's death! – us'd thee.

**Desdemona**
How? unlawfully?

**Othello**
           Ay.

**Desdemona**
He will not say so.

**Othello**
           No, his mouth is stopp'd;
Honest Iago hath ta'en order for't.                            75

**Desdemona**
O, my fear interprets! What, is he dead?

**Othello**
Had all his hairs been lives, my great revenge
Had stomach for them all.

**Desdemona**
Alas, he is betray'd, and I undone!

**Othello**
Out, strumpet! Weep'st thou for him to my face?               80

**Desdemona**
O, banish me, my lord, but kill me not!

*Othello*
Down, strumpet.

*Desdemona*
Kill me to-morrow; let me live to-night.

*Othello*
Nay, an you strive –

*Desdemona*
85 But half an hour!

*Othello*
Being done, there is no pause.

*Desdemona*
But while I say one prayer!

*Othello*
It is too late.   *[Smothers her.]*

*Desdemona*
O lord, Lord, Lord!

*Emilia*
*[Within]* My lord, my lord! what, ho! my lord, my
90    lord!

*Othello*
What voice is this? Not dead? not yet quite dead?
I that am cruel am yet merciful;
I would not have thee linger in thy pain.
So, so.

*Emilia*
95 *[Within]* What, ho! my lord, my lord!

*Othello*
Who's there?

*Emilia*
*[Within]* O, good my lord, I'd speak a word with
    you!

*Othello*
Yes – 'tis Emilia – by and by. She's dead.
'Tis like she comes to speak of Cassio's death;
100   The noise was high. Ha! no more moving?
Still as the grave. Shall she come in? Were't good?
I think she stirs again. No. What's the best?

If she come in she'll sure speak to my wife.
My wife! my wife! what wife? I have no wife.
O insupportable! O heavy hour!                              105
Methinks it should be now a huge eclipse
Of sun and moon, and that th' affrighted globe
Did yawn at alteration.

**Emilia**

[Within] I do beseech you that I may speak with you.
    O good my lord!

**Othello**

I had forgot thee: O, come in, Emilia.                     110
Soft, by and by. Let me the curtains draw.
Where art thou?

                    [Unlocks the door.]

                    [Enter EMILIA.]

                    What's the matter with thee now?

**Emilia**

O, my good lord, yonder's foul murders done!

**Othello**

What, now?

**Emilia**

But now, my lord.                                          115

**Othello**

It is the very error of the moon;
She comes more nearer earth than she was wont,
And makes men mad.

**Emilia**

Cassio, my lord, hath kill'd a young Venetian
Call'd Roderigo.

**Othello**

                    Roderigo kill'd!                        120
And Cassio kill'd!

**Emilia**

                    No, Cassio, is not kill'd.

*Othello*
> Not Cassio kill'd! Then murder's out of tune,
> And sweet revenge grows harsh.

*Desdemona*
> O, falsely, falsely murder'd!

*Emilia*
>                              O Lord, what cry is that?

*Othello*
125   That! what?

*Emilia*
> Out and alas! that was my lady's voice.
> Help! help, ho! help! O lady, speak again!
> Sweet Desdemona! O sweet mistress, speak!

*Desdemona*
> A guiltless death I die.

*Emilia*
130   O, who hath done this deed?

*Desdemona*
> Nobody. I myself. Farewell.
> Commend me to my kind lord. O, farewell!

> *[She dies.]*

*Othello*
> Why, how should she be murd'red?

*Emilia*
>                              Alas, who knows?

*Othello*
> You heard her say herself it was not I.

*Emilia*
135   She said so. I must needs report a truth.

*Othello*
> She's like a liar gone to burning hell:
> 'Twas I that kill'd her.

*Emilia*
>                    O, the more angel she,
> And you the blacker devil!

**Othello**
  She turn'd to folly, and she was a whore.
**Emilia**
  Thou dost belie her, and thou art a devil.                    140
**Othello**
  She was false as water.
**Emilia**
                    Thou art rash as fire to say
  That she was false. O, she was heavenly true!
**Othello**
  Cassio did top her; ask thy husband else.
  O, I were damn'd beneath all depth in hell
  But that I did proceed upon just grounds        145
  To this extremity. Thy husband knew it all.
**Emilia**
  My husband!
**Othello**
  Thy husband.
**Emilia**
  That she was false to wedlock?
**Othello**
  Ay, with Cassio. Nay, had she been true,        150
  If heaven would make me such another world
  Of one entire and perfect chrysolite,
  I'd not have sold her for it.
**Emilia**
  My husband!
**Othello**
  Ay, 'twas he that told me on her first.        155
  An honest man he is, and hates the slime
  That sticks on filthy deeds.
**Emilia**
                    My husband!
**Othello**
  What needs this iterance, woman? I say thy
    husband.

*Emilia*
> O mistress, villainy hath made mocks with love!
> My husband say that she was false!

*Othello*
160                                     He, woman;
> I say thy husband; dost understand the word?
> My friend, thy husband – honest, honest Iago.

*Emilia*
> If he say so, may his pernicious soul
> Rot half a grain a day! He lies to th' heart.
165  She was too fond of her most filthy bargain.

*Othello*
> Ha!

*Emilia*
> Do thy worst:
> This deed of thine is no more worthy heaven
> Than thou wast worthy her.

*Othello*
                             Peace, you were best.

*Emilia*
170  Thou hast not half that power to do me harm
> As I have to be hurt. O gull! O dolt!
> As ignorant as dirt! Thou hast done a deed –
> I care not for thy sword; I'll make thee known,
> Though I lost twenty lives. Help! help, ho! help!
175  The Moor hath kill'd my mistress! Murder! murder!

*[Enter MONTANO, GRATIANO, IAGO, and Others.]*

*Montano*
> What is the matter? How now, General!

*Emilia*
> O, are you come, Iago? You have done well,
> That men must lay their murders on your neck.

*Gratiano*
> What is the matter?

*Emilia*
180  Disprove this villain, if thou be'st a man:

He says thou told'st him that his wife was false.
I know thou didst not; thou'rt not such a villain.
Speak, for my heart is full.

*Iago*

I told him what I thought, and told no more
Than what he found himself was apt and true.          185

*Emilia*

But did you ever tell him she was false?

*Iago*

I did.

*Emilia*

You told a lie – an odious, damned lie.
Upon my soul, a lie – a wicked lie.
She false with Cassio! Did you say with Cassio?          190

*Iago*

With Cassio, mistress. Go to, charm your tongue.

*Emilia*

I will not charm my tongue; I am bound to speak:
My mistress here lies murdered in her bed.

*All*

O heavens forfend!

*Emilia*

And your reports have set the murder on.          195

*Othello*

Nay, stare not, masters: it is true, indeed.

*Gratiano*

'Tis a strange truth.

*Montano*

                    O monstrous act!

*Emilia*

Villainy, villainy, villainy!
I think upon't. I think – I smell't. villainy!
I thought so then. I'll kill myself for grief.          200
O villainy, villainy!

*Iago*

What, are you mad? I charge you get you home.

*Emilia*
    Good gentlemen, let me have leave to speak.
    'Tis proper I obey him, but not now.
205    Perchance, Iago, I will ne'er go home.
*Othello*
    O! O! O! *[Falls on the bed.]*
*Emilia*
             Nay, lay thee down and roar;
    For thou hast kill'd the sweetest innocent
    That e'er did lift up eye.
*Othello*
    *[Rising]*          O, she was foul!
    I scarce did know you, uncle. There lies your niece,
210    Whose breath indeed these hands have newly
        stopp'd.
    I know this act shows horrible and grim.
*Gratiano*
    Poor Desdemona! I am glad thy father's dead.
    Thy match was mortal to him, and pure grief
    Shore his old thread atwain. Did he live now,
215    This sight would make him do a desperate turn,
    Yea, curse his better angel from his side,
    And fall to reprobance.
*Othello*
    'Tis pitiful; but yet Iago knows
    That she with Cassio hath the act of shame
220    A thousand times committed; Cassio confess'd it;
    And she did gratify his amorous works
    With that recognizance and pledge of love
    Which I first gave her; I saw it in his hand.
    It was a handkerchief, an antique token
225    My father gave my mother.
*Emilia*
    O God! O heavenly God!
*Iago*
    Zounds, hold your peace.

*Emilia*
'Twill out, 'twill out. I, peace!
No, I will speak as liberal as the north.
Let heaven and men and devils, let them all,    230
All, all, cry shame against me, yet I'll speak.

*Iago*
Be wise, and get you home.

*Emilia*
                I will not.

*[IAGO offers to stab his wife.]*

*Gratiano*
Fie! Your sword upon a woman?

*Emilia*
O thou dull Moor! That handkerchief thou speak'st
  of
I found by fortune, and did give my husband;   235
For often with a solemn earnestness –
More than indeed belong'd to such a trifle –
He begg'd of me to steal it.

*Iago*
             Villainous whore!

*Emilia*
She give it Cassio! No, alas, I found it,
And I did give't my husband.

*Iago*
             Filth, thou liest.   240

*Emilia*
By heaven, I do not, I do not, gentlemen.
O murderous coxcomb! What should such a fool
Do with so good a wife? *[The Moor runs at* IAGO*;*
    MONTANO *and others disarm the Moor.* IAGO *kills his*
    *wife and escapes.]*

*Othello*
Are there no stones in heaven but what serves for the
thunder? Precious villain!   245

*Gratiano*
　The woman falls; sure he hath kill'd his wife.
*Emilia*
　Ay, ay. O, lay me by my mistress' side.
*Gratiano*
　He's gone, but his wife's kill'd.
*Montano*
　'Tis a notorious villain. Take you this weapon,
250　Which I have here recover'd from the Moor.
　Come, guard the door without; let him not pass,
　But kill him rather. I'll after that same villain,
　For 'tis a damned slave.

　　　*[Exeunt MONTANO, GRATIANO, and others.]*

*Othello*
　I am not valiant neither –
255　But every puny whipster gets my sword.
　But why should honour outlive honesty?
　Let it go all.
*Emilia*
　What did thy song bode, lady?
　Hark, canst thou hear me? I will play the swan,
260　And die in music. *[Sings]* Willow, willow, willow. –
　Moor, she was chaste; she lov'd thee, cruel Moor;
　So come my soul to bliss, as I speak true;
　So speaking as I think, alas, I die.

　　　*[She dies.]*

*Othello*
　I have another weapon in this chamber;
265　It was a sword of Spain, the ice-brook's temper.
　O, here it is. Uncle, I must come forth.
*Gratiano*
　*[Within]* If thou attempt it, it will cost thee dear;
　Thou hast no weapon, and perforce must suffer.
*Othello*
　Look in upon me, then, and speak with me,
270　Or, naked as I am, I will assault thee.

*[Re-enter* GRATIANO.*]*

**Gratiano**
   What is the matter?
**Othello**
                    Behold, I have a weapon;
   A better never did itself sustain
   Upon a soldier's thigh. I have seen the day
   That with this little arm and this good sword
   I have made my way through more impediments          275
   Than twenty times your stop. But, O vain boast!
   Who can control his fate? 'Tis not so now.
   Be not afraid though you do see me weapon'd;
   Here is my journey's end, here is my butt,
   And very sea-mark of my utmost sail.                 280
   Do you go back dismay'd? 'Tis a lost fear;
   Man but a rush against Othello's breast,
   And he retires. Where should Othello go?
   Now, how dost thou look now? O ill-starr'd wench!
   Pale as thy smock! When we shall meet at compt,      285
   This look of thine will hurl my soul from heaven,
   And fiends will snatch at it. Cold, cold, my girl!
   Even like thy chastity. O cursed, cursed slave!
   Whip me, ye devils,
   From the possession of this heavenly sight.          290
   Blow me about in winds, roast me in sulphur,
   Wash me in steep-down gulfs of liquid fire.
   O Desdemona! Dead! Desdemona! Dead!
   O! O!

      *[Enter* LODOVICO, MONTANO, CASSIO *carried in a
          chair, and Officers, with* IAGO *prisoner.]*

**Lodovico**
   Where is this rash and most unfortunate man?         295
**Othello**
   That's he that was Othello – here I am.
**Lodovico**
   Where is that viper? Bring the villain forth.

*Othello*
> I look down towards his feet – but that's a fable.
> If that thou be'st a devil, I cannot kill thee.

*[Wounds* IAGO.*]*

*Lodovico*
300    Wrench his sword from him.

*Iago*
> I bleed, sir; but not kill'd.

*Othello*
> I am not sorry neither: I'd have thee live;
> For, in my sense, 'tis happiness to die.

*Lodovico*
> O thou Othello, that was once so good,
305    Fall'n in the practice of a damned slave,
> What shall be said to thee?

*Othello*
>                   Why, any thing:
> An honourable murderer, if you will;
> For nought I did in hate, but all in honour.

*Lodovico*
> This wretch hath part confess'd his villainy.
310    Did you and he consent in Cassio's death?

*Othello*
> Ay.

*Cassio*
> Dear General, I never gave you cause.

*Othello*
> I do believe it, and I ask your pardon.
> Will you, I pray, demand that demi-devil
315    Why he hath thus ensnar'd my soul and body?

*Iago*
> Demand me nothing. What you know, you know.
> From this time forth I never will speak word.

*Lodovico*
> What, not to pray?

**Gratiano**

              Torments will ope your lips.

**Othello**

  Well, thou dost best.

**Lodovico**

  Sir, you shall understand what hath befall'n,      320
  Which, as I think, you know not. Here is a letter
  Found in the pocket of the slain Roderigo;
  And here another: the one of them imports
  The death of Cassio to be undertook
  By Roderigo.      325

**Othello**

  O villain!

**Cassio**

          Most heathenish and most gross!

**Lodovico**

  Now here's another discontented paper,
  Found in his pocket too; and this, it seems,
  Roderigo meant t' have sent this damned villain;
  But that, belike, Iago in the nick      330
  Came in and satisfied him.

**Othello**

              O thou pernicious caitiff!
  How came you, Cassio, by that handkerchief
  That was my wife's?

**Cassio**

          I found it in my chamber;
  And he himself confess'd it even now
  That there he dropp'd it for a special purpose      335
  Which wrought to his desire.

**Othello**

             O fool! fool! fool!

**Cassio**

  There is besides in Roderigo's letter,
  How he upbraids Iago that he made him
  Brave me upon the watch; whereon it came
  That I was cast; and even but now he spake,      340

After long seeming dead, Iago hurt him,
Iago set him on.

Lodovico

You must forsake this room and go with us.
Your power and your command is taken off,
345 And Cassio rules in Cyprus. For this slave,
If there be any cunning cruelty
That can torment him much and hold him long,
It shall be his. You shall close prisoner rest
Till that the nature of your fault be known
350 To the Venetian state. Come, bring away.

Othello

Soft you; a word or two before you go.
I have done the state some service, and they know't –
No more of that. I pray you, in your letters,
When you shall these unlucky deeds relate,
355 Speak of me as I am; nothing extenuate,
Nor set down aught in malice. Then must you speak
Of one that lov'd not wisely, but too well;
Of one not easily jealous, but, being wrought,
Perplexed in the extreme; of one whose hand,
360 Like the base Indian, threw a pearl away
Richer than all his tribe; one of whose subdu'd eyes,
Albeit unused to the melting mood,
Drops tears as fast as the Arabian trees
Their med'cinable gum. Set you down this:
365 And say besides that in Aleppo once,
Where a malignant and a turban'd Turk
Beat a Venetian and traduc'd the state,
I took by th' throat the circumcised dog,
And smote him – thus.

*[He stabs himself.]*

Lodovico

O bloody period!

Gratiano

370            All that is spoke is marr'd.

*Othello*
 I kiss'd thee ere I kill'd thee. No way but this –
 Killing my self, to die upon a kiss.

   *[Falls on the bed and dies.]*

*Cassio*
 This did I fear, but thought he had no weapon;
 For he was great of heart.

*Lodovico*
 *[To* IAGO*]*    O Spartan dog,
 More fell than anguish, hunger, or the sea!   375
 Look on the tragic loading of this bed.
 This is thy work. – The object poisons sight;
 Let it be hid. Gratiano, keep the house,
 And seize upon the fortunes of the Moor,
 For they succeed on you. To you, Lord Governor,  380
 Remains the censure of this hellish villain;
 The time, the place, the torture – O, enforce it!
 Myself will straight aboard; and to the state
 This heavy act with heavy heart relate. *[Exeunt.]*

# Shakespeare: Words and Phrases

*adapted from the Collins English Dictionary*

**abate** 1 VERB to abate here means to lessen or diminish ❏ *There lives within the very flame of love/A kind of wick or snuff that will abate it* (*Hamlet 4.7*) 2 VERB to abate here means to shorten ❏ *Abate thy hours* (*A Midsummer Night's Dream 3.2*) 3 VERB to abate here means to deprive ❏ *She hath abated me of half my train* (*King Lear 2.4*)

**abjure** VERB to abjure means to renounce or give up ❏ *this rough magic I here abjure* (*Tempest 5.1*)

**abroad** ADV abroad means elsewhere or everywhere ❏ *You have heard of the news abroad* (*King Lear 2.1*)

**abrogate** VERB to abrogate means to put an end to ❏ *so it shall praise you to abrogate scurrility* (*Love's Labours Lost 4.2*)

**abuse** 1 NOUN abuse in this context means deception or fraud ❏ *What should this mean? Are all the rest come back?/Or is it some abuse, and no such thing?* (*Hamlet 4.7*) 2 NOUN an abuse in this context means insult or offence ❏ *I will be deaf to pleading and excuses/Nor tears nor prayers shall purchase our abuses* (*Romeo and Juliet 3.1*) 3 NOUN an abuse in this context means using something improperly ❏ *we'll digest/Th'abuse*

of distance (*Henry II Chorus*) 4 NOUN an abuse in this context means doing something which is corrupt or dishonest ❏ *Come, bring them away: if these be good people in a commonweal that do nothing but their abuses in common houses, I know no law: bring them away.* (*Measure for Measure 2.1*)

**abuser** NOUN the abuser here is someone who betrays, a betrayer ❏ *I ... do attach thee/For an abuser of the world* (*Othello 1.2*)

**accent** NOUN accent here means language ❏ *In states unborn, and accents yet unknown* (*Julius Caesar 3.1*)

**accident** NOUN an accident in this context is an event or something that happened ❏ *think no more of this night's accidents* (*A Midsummer Night's Dream 4.1*)

**accommodate** VERB to accommodate in this context means to equip or to give someone the equipment to do something ❏ *The safer sense will ne'er accommodate/His master thus.* (*King Lear 4.6*)

**according** ADJ according means sympathetic or ready to agree ❏ *within the scope of choice/Lies*

my consent and fair according voice
(*Romeo and Juliet* 1.2)

**account** NOUN account often means
judgement (by God) or reckoning
❏ *No reckoning made, but sent to my
account/With all my imperfections on
my head* (*Hamlet* 1.5)

**accountant** ADJ accountant here
means answerable or accountable
❏ *his offence is… /Accountant to the
law* (*Measure for Measure* 2.4)

**ace** NOUN ace here means one or first
referring to the lowest score on a dice
❏ *No die, but an ace, for him; for he is
but one./Less than an ace, man; for he
is dead; he is nothing.* (*A Midsummer
Night's Dream* 5.1)

**acquit** VERB here acquit means to be
rid of or free of. It is related to the
verb quit ❏ *I am glad I am so acquit
of this tinderbox* (*The Merry Wives of
Windsor* 1.3)

**afeard** ADJ afeard means afraid or
frightened ❏ *Nothing afeard of what
thyself didst make* (*Macbeth* 1.3)

**affiance** NOUN affiance means
confidence or trust ❏ *O how hast
thou with jealousy infected/The
sweetness of affiance* (*Henry V* 2.2)

**affinity** NOUN in this context, affinity
means important connections, or
relationships with important people
❏ *The Moor replies/That he you hurt
is of great fame in Cyprus,/And great
affinity* (*Othello* 3.1)

**agnize** VERB to agnize is an old
word that means that you recognize
or acknowledge something ❏ *I do
agnize/A natural and prompt alacrity
I find in hardness* (*Othello* 1.3)

**ague** NOUN an ague is a fever in
which the patient has hot and cold

shivers one after the other ❏ *This
is some monster of the isle with four
legs, who hath got … an ague* (*The
Tempest* 2.2)

**alarm, alarum** NOUN an alarm or
alarum is a call to arms or a signal for
soldiers to prepare to fight ❏ *Whence
cometh this alarum and the noise?*
(*Henry VI part I* 1.4)

**Albion** NOUN Albion is another
word for England ❏ *but I will sell my
dukedom,/To buy a slobbery and a
dirty farm In that nook-shotten isle of
Albion* (*Henry V* 3.5)

**all of all** PHRASE all of all means
everything, or the sum of all things
❏ *The very all of all* (*Love's Labours
Lost* 5.1)

**amend** VERB amend in this context
means to get better or to heal ❏ *at
his touch… They presently amend*
(*Macbeth* 4.3)

**anchor** VERB if you anchor on
something you concentrate on it or
fix on it ❏ *My invention ... Anchors
on Isabel* (*Measure for Measure* 2.4)

**anon** ADV anon was a common word
for soon ❏ *You shall see anon how the
murderer gets the love of Gonzago's
wife* (*Hamlet* 3.2)

**antic** 1 ADJ antic here means weird
or strange ❏ *I'll charm the air to give
a sound/While you perform your antic
round* (*Macbeth* 4.1) 2 NOUN in
this context antic means a clown or
a strange, unattractive creature ❏ *If
black, why nature, drawing an antic,/
Made a foul blot* (*Much Ado About
Nothing* 3.1)

**apace** ADV apace was a common word
for quickly ❏ *Come apace* (*As You
Like It* 3.3)

**apparel** NOUN apparel means clothes or clothing ❑ *one suit of apparel* (*Hamlet 3.2*)

**appliance** NOUN appliance here means cure ❑ *Diseases desperate grown/ By desperate appliance are relieved* (*Hamlet 4.3*)

**argument** NOUN argument here means a topic of conversation or the subject ❑ *Why 'tis the rarest argument of wonder that hath shot out in our latter times* (*All's Well That Ends Well 2.3*)

**arrant** ADJ arrant means absolute, complete. It strengthens the meaning of a noun ❑ *Fortune, that arrant whore* (*King Lear 2.4*)

**arras** NOUN an arras is a tapestry, a large cloth with a picture sewn on it using coloured thread ❑ *Behind the arras I'll convey myself/ To hear the process* (*Hamlet 3.3*)

**art** 1 NOUN art in this context means knowledge ❑ *Their malady convinces/ The great essay of art* (*Macbeth 4.3*) 2 NOUN art can also mean skill as it does here ❑ *He ... gave you such a masterly report/ For art and exercise in your defence* (*Hamlet 4.7*) 3 NOUN art here means magic ❑ *Now I want/ Spirits to enforce, art to enchant* (*The Tempest 5 Epilogue*)

**assay** 1 NOUN an assay was an attempt, a try ❑ *Make assay./ Bow, stubborn knees* (*Hamlet 3.3*) 2 NOUN assay can also mean a test or a trial ❑ *he hath made assay of her virtue* (*Measure for Measure 3.1*)

**attend (on/upon)** VERB attend on means to wait for or to expect ❑ *Tarry I here, I but attend on death* (*Two Gentlemen of Verona 3.1*)

**auditor** NOUN an auditor was a member of an audience or someone who listens ❑ *I'll be an auditor* (*A Midsummer Night's Dream 3.1*)

**aught** NOUN aught was a common word which meant anything ❑ *if my love thou holdest at aught* (*Hamlet 4.3*)

**aunt** 1 NOUN an aunt was another word for an old woman and also means someone who talks a lot or a gossip ❑ *The wisest aunt telling the saddest tale* (*A Midsummer Night's Dream 2.1*) 2 NOUN aunt could also mean a mistress or a prostitute ❑ *the thrush and the jay/ Are summer songs for me and my aunts/ While we lie tumbling in the hay* (*The Winter's Tale 4.3*)

**avaunt** EXCLAM avaunt was a common word which meant go away ❑ *Avaunt, you curs!* (*King Lear 3.6*)

**aye** ADV here aye means always or ever ❑ *Whose state and honour I for aye allow* (*Richard II 5.2*)

**baffle** VERB baffle meant to be disgraced in public or humiliated ❑ *I am disgraced, impeached, and baffled here* (*Richard II 1.1*)

**bald** ADJ bald means trivial or silly ❑ *I knew 'twould be a bald conclusion* (*The Comedy of Errors 2.2*)

**ban** NOUN a ban was a curse or an evil spell ❑ *Sometimes with lunatic bans... Enforce their charity* (*King Lear 2.3*)

**barren** ADJ barren meant empty or hollow ❑ *now I let go your hand, I am barren.* (*Twelfth Night 1.3*)

**base** ADJ base is an adjective that means unworthy or dishonourable ❑ *civit is of a baser birth than tar* (*As You Like It 3.2*)

**base** 1 ADJ base can also mean of low social standing or someone who was not part of the ruling class ❏ *Why brand they us with 'base'?* (*King Lear* 1.2) 2 ADJ here base means poor quality ❏ *Base cousin,/ Darest thou break first?* (*Two Noble Kinsmen* 3.3)

**bawdy** NOUN bawdy means obscene or rude ❏ *Bloody, bawdy villain!* (*Hamlet* 2.2)

**bear in hand** PHRASE bear in hand means taken advantage of or fooled ❏ *This I made good to you In our last conference, passed in probation with you/ How you were borne in hand* (*Macbeth* 3.1)

**beard** VERB to beard someone was to oppose or confront them ❏ *Com'st thou to beard me in Denmark?* (*Hamlet* 2.2)

**beard, in one's** PHRASE if you say something in someone's beard you say it to their face ❏ *I will verify as much in his beard* (*Henry V* 3.2)

**beaver** NOUN a beaver was a visor on a battle helmet ❏ *O yes, my lord, he wore his beaver up* (*Hamlet* 1.2)

**become** VERB if something becomes you it suits you or is appropriate to you ❏ *Nothing in his life became him like the leaving it* (*Macbeth* 1.4)

**bed, brought to** PHRASE to be brought to bed means to give birth ❏ *His wife but yesternight was brought to bed* (*Titus Andronicus* 4.2)

**bedabbled** ADJ if something is bedabbled it is sprinkled ❏ *Bedabbled with the dew, and torn with briers* (*A Midsummer Night's Dream* 3.2)

**Bedlam** NOUN Bedlam was a word used for Bethlehem Hospital which was a place the insane were sent to ❏ *The country give me proof and precedent/ Of Bedlam beggars* (*King Lear* 2.3)

**bed-swerver** NOUN a bed-swerver was someone who was unfaithful in marriage, an adulterer ❏ *she's/ A bed-swerver* (*Winter's Tale* 2.1)

**befall** 1 VERB to befall is to happen, occur or take place ❏ *In this same interlude it doth befall/ That I present a wall* (*A Midsummer Night's Dream* 5.1) 2 VERB to befall can also mean to happen to someone or something ❏ *fair befall thee and thy noble house* (*Richard III* 1.3)

**behoof** NOUN behoof was an advantage or benefit ❏ *All our surgeons/ Convent in their behoof* (*Two Noble Kinsmen* 1.4)

**beldam** NOUN a beldam was a witch or old woman ❏ *Have I not reason, beldams as you are?* (*Macbeth* 3.5)

**belike** ADV belike meant probably, perhaps or presumably ❏ *belike he likes it not* (*Hamlet* 3.2)

**bent** 1 NOUN bent means a preference or a direction ❏ *Let me work,/ For I can give his humour true bent,/ And I will bring him to the Capitol* (*Julius Caesar* 2.1) 2 ADJ if you are bent on something you are determined to do it ❏ *for now I am bent to know/ By the worst means the worst.* (*Macbeth* 3.4)

**beshrew** VERB beshrew meant to curse or wish evil on someone ❏ *much beshrew my manners and my pride/ If Hermia meant to say Lysander lied* (*A Midsummer Night's Dream* 2.2)

**betime (s)** ADV betime means early ❏ *To business that we love we rise betime* (Antony and Cleopatra 4.4)

**bevy** NOUN bevy meant type or sort, it was also used to mean company ❏ *many more of the same bevy* (Hamlet 5.2)

**blazon** VERB to blazon something meant to display or show it ❏ *that thy skill be more to blazon it* (Romeo and Juliet 2.6)

**blind** ADJ if you are blind when you do something you are reckless or do not care about the consequences ❏ *are you yet to your own souls so blind/ That two you will war with God by murdering me* (Richard III 1.4)

**bombast** NOUN bombast was wool stuffing (used in a cushion for example) and so it came to mean padded out or long-winded. Here it means someone who talks a lot about nothing in particular ❏ *How now my sweet creature of bombast* (Henry IV part I 2.4)

**bond** 1 NOUN a bond is a contract or legal deed ❏ *Well, then, your bond, and let me see* (Merchant of Venice 1.3) 2 NOUN bond could also mean duty or commitment ❏ *I love your majesty/ According to my bond* (King Lear 1.1)

**bottom** NOUN here bottom means essence, main point or intent ❏ *Now I see/ The bottom of your purpose* (All's Well That Ends Well 3.7)

**bounteously** ADV bounteously means plentifully, abundantly ❏ *I prithee, and I'll pay thee bounteously* (Twelfth Night 1.2)

**brace** 1 NOUN a brace is a couple or two ❏ *Have lost a brace of kinsmen* (Romeo and Juliet 5.3) 2 NOUN if you are in a brace position it means you are ready ❏ *For that it stands not in such warlike brace* (Othello 1.3)

**brand** VERB to mark permanently like the markings on cattle ❏ *the wheeled seat/ Of fortunate Caesar ... branded his baseness that ensued* (Anthony and Cleopatra 4.14)

**brave** ADJ brave meant fine, excellent or splendid ❏ *O brave new world/ That has such people in't* (The Tempest 5.1)

**brine** NOUN brine is sea-water ❏ *He shall drink nought brine, for I'll not show him/ Where the quick freshes are* (The Tempest 3.2)

**brow** NOUN brow in this context means appearance ❏ *doth hourly grow/ Out of his brows* (Hamlet 3.3)

**burden** 1 NOUN the burden here is a chorus ❏ *I would sing my song without a burden* (As You Like It 3.2) 2 NOUN burden means load or weight (this is the current meaning) ❏ *the scarfs and the bannerets about thee did manifoldly dissuade me from believing thee a vessel of too great a burden* (All's Well that Ends Well 2.3)

**buttons, in one's** PHRASE this is a phrase that means clear, easy to see ❏ *Tis in his buttons he will carry't* (The Merry Wives of Windsor 3.2)

**cable** NOUN cable here means scope or reach ❏ *The law ... Will give her cable* (Othello 1.2)

**cadent** ADJ if something is cadent it is falling or dropping ❏ *With cadent tears fret channels in her cheeks* (King Lear 1.4)

**canker** VERB to canker is to decay, become corrupt ❏ *And, as with age his body uglier grows,/So his mind cankers* (The Tempest 4.1)

**canon, from the** PHRASE from the canon is an expression meaning out of order, improper ❏ *Twas from the canon* (Coriolanus 3.1)

**cap-a-pie** ADV cap-a-pie means from head to foot, completely ❏ *I am courtier cap-a-pie* (The Winter's Tale 4.4)

**carbonadoed** ADJ if something is carbonadoed it is cut or scored (scratched) with a knife ❏ *it is your carbonadoed* (All's Well That Ends Well 4.5)

**carouse** VERB to carouse is to drink at length, party ❏ *They cast their caps up and carouse together* (Anthony and Cleopatra 4.12)

**carrack** NOUN a carrack was a large old ship, a galleon ❏ *Faith, he tonight hath boarded a land-carrack* (Othello 1.2)

**cassock** NOUN a cassock here means a military cloak, long coat ❏ *half of the which dare not shake the snow from off their cassocks lest they shake themselves to pieces* (All's Well That Ends Well 4.3)

**catastrophe** NOUN catastrophe here means conclusion or end ❏ *pat he comes, like the catastrophe of the old comedy* (King Lear 1.2)

**cautel** NOUN a cautel was a trick or a deceptive act ❏ *Perhaps he loves you now/And now no soil not cautel doth besmirch* (Hamlet 1.2)

**celerity** NOUN celerity was a common word for speed, swiftness ❏ *Hence hath offence his quick celerity/When it is borne in high authority* (Measure for Measure 4.2)

**chafe** NOUN chafe meant anger or temper ❏ *this Herculean Roman does become/The carriage of his chafe* (Anthony and Cleopatra 1.3)

**chanson** NOUN chanson was an old word for a song ❏ *The first row of the pious chanson will show you more* (Hamlet 2.2)

**chapman** NOUN a chapman was a trader or merchant ❏ *Not uttered by base sale of chapman's tongues* (Love's Labours Lost 2.1)

**chaps, chops** NOUN chaps (and chops) was a word for jaws ❏ *Which ne'er shook hands nor bade farewell to him/Till he unseamed him from the nave to th' chops* (Macbeth 1.2)

**chattels** NOUN chattels were your moveable possessions. The word is used in the traditional marriage ceremony ❏ *She is my goods, my chattels* (The Taming of the Shrew 3.3)

**chide** VERB if you are chided by someone you are told off or reprimanded ❏ *Now I but chide, but I should use thee worse* (A Midsummer Night's Dream 3.2)

**chinks** NOUN chinks was a word for cash or money ❏ *he that can lay hold of her/Shall have the chinks* (Romeo and Juliet 1.5)

**choleric** ADJ if something was called choleric it meant that they were quick to get angry ❏ *therewithal unruly waywardness that infirm and choleric years bring with them* (King Lear 1.1)

**chuff** NOUN a chuff was a miser,

someone who clings to his or her money ❏ *ye fat chuffs* (*Henry IV part I 2.2*)

**cipher** NOUN cipher here means nothing ❏ *Mine were the very cipher of a function* (*Measure for Measure 2.2*)

**circummured** ADJ circummured means that something is surrounded with a wall ❏ *He hath a garden circummured with brick* (*Measure for Measure 4.1*)

**civet** NOUN a civet is a type of scent or perfume ❏ *Give me an ounce of civet* (*King Lear 4.6*)

**clamorous** ADJ clamorous means noisy or boisterous ❏ *Be clamorous and leap all civil bounds* (*Twelfth Night 1.4*)

**clangour, clangor** NOUN clangour is a word that means ringing (the sound that bells make) ❏ *Like to a dismal clangour heard from far* (*Henry VI part III 2.3*)

**cleave** VERB if you cleave to something you stick to it or are faithful to it ❏ *Thy thoughts I cleave to* (*The Tempest 4.1*)

**clock and clock, 'twixt** PHRASE from hour to hour, without stopping or continuously ❏ *To weep 'twixt clock and clock* (*Cymbeline 3.4*)

**close** ADJ here close means hidden ❏ *Stand close; this is the same Athenian* (*A Midsummer Night's Dream 3.2*)

**cloud** NOUN a cloud on your face means that you have a troubled, unhappy expression ❏ *He has cloud in's face* (*Anthony and Cleopatra 3.2*)

**cloy** VERB if you cloy an appetite you satisfy it ❏ *Other women cloy/The*

*appetites they feed* (*Anthony and Cleopatra 2.2*)

**cock-a-hoop, set** PHRASE if you set cock-a-hoop you become free of everything ❏ *You will set cock-a-hoop* (*Romeo and Juliet 1.5*)

**colours** NOUN colours is a word used to describe battle-flags or banners. Sometimes we still say that we nail our colours to the mast if we are stating which team or side of an argument we support ❏ *the approbation of those that weep this lamentable divorce under her colours* (*Cymbeline 1.5*)

**combustion** NOUN combustion was a word meaning disorder or chaos ❏ *prophesying ... Of dire combustion and confused events* (*Macbeth 2.3*)

**comely** ADJ if you are or something is comely you or it is lovely, beautiful, graceful ❏ *O, what a world is this, when what is comely/Envenoms him that bears it!* (*As You Like It 2.3*)

**commend** VERB if you commend yourself to someone you send greetings to them ❏ *Commend me to my brother* (*Measure for Measure 1.4*)

**compact** NOUN a compact is an agreement or a contract ❏ *what compact mean you to have with us?* (*Julius Caesar 3.1*)

**compass** 1 NOUN here compass means range or scope ❏ *you would sound me from my lowest note to the top of my compass* (*Hamlet 3.2*) 2 VERB to compass here means to achieve, bring about or make happen ❏ *How now shall this be compassed?/ Canst thou bring me to the party?* (*Tempest 3.2*)

**comptible** ADJ comptible is an old word meaning sensitive ❑ *I am very comptible, even to the least sinister usage.* (*Twelfth Night 1.5*)

**confederacy** NOUN a confederacy is a group of people usually joined together to commit a crime. It is another word for a conspiracy ❑ *Lo, she is one of this confederacy!* (*A Midsummer Night's Dream 3.2*)

**confound** VERB if you confound something you confuse it or mix it up; it also means to stop or prevent ❑ *A million fail, confounding oath on oath.* (*A Midsummer Night's Dream 3.2*)

**contagion** NOUN contagion is an old word for disease or poison ❑ *hell itself breathes out/ Contagion to this world* (*Hamlet 3.2*)

**contumely** NOUN contumely is an old word for an insult ❑ *the proud man's contumely* (*Hamlet 3.1*)

**counterfeit** 1 VERB if you counterfeit something you copy or imitate it ❑ *Meantime your cheeks do counterfeit our roses* (*Henry VI part I 2.4*) 2 VERB in this context counterfeit means to pretend or make believe ❑ *I will counterfeit the bewitchment of some popular man* (*Coriolanus*)

**coz** NOUN coz was a shortened form of the word cousin ❑ *sweet my coz, be merry* (*As You Like It 1.2*)

**cozenage** NOUN cozenage is an old word meaning cheating or a deception ❑ *Thrown out his angle for my proper life,/ And with such coz'nage* (*Hamlet 5.2*)

**crave** VERB crave used to mean to beg or request ❑ *I crave your pardon* (*The Comedy of Errors 1.2*)

**crotchet** NOUN crotchets are strange ideas or whims ❑ *thou hast some strange crotchets in thy head now* (*The Merry Wives of Windsor 2.1*)

**cuckold** NOUN a cuckold is a man whose wife has been unfaithful to him ❑ *As there is no true cuckold but calamity* (*Twelfth Night 1.5*)

**cuffs, go to** PHRASE this phrase meant to fight ❑ *the player went to cuffs in the question* (*Hamlet 2.2*)

**cup** VERB in this context cup is a verb which means to pour drink or fill glasses with alcohol ❑ *cup us til the world go round* (*Anthony and Cleopatra 2.7*)

**cur** NOUN cur is an insult meaning dog and is also used to mean coward ❑ *Out, dog! out, cur! Thou drivest me past the bounds/ Of maiden's patience* (*A Midsummer Night's Dream 3.2*)

**curiously** ADV in this context curiously means carefully or skilfully ❑ *The sleeves curiously cut* (*The Taming of the Shrew 4.3*)

**curry** VERB curry means to flatter or to praise someone more than they are worth ❑ *I would curry with Master Shallow that no man could better command his servants* (*Henry IV part II 5.1*)

**custom** NOUN custom is a habit or a usual practice ❑ *Hath not old custom made this life more sweet/ Than that of painted pomp?* (*As You Like It 2.1*)

**cutpurse** NOUN a cutpurse is an old word for a thief. Men used to carry their money in small bags (purse) that hung from their belts; thieves would cut the purse from the belt and steal their money ❑ *A cutpurse of the empire and the rule* (*Hamlet 3.4*)

**dainty** ADJ dainty used to mean splendid, fine ❑ *Why, that's my dainty Ariel!* (*Tempest* 5.1)

**dally** VERB if you dally with something you play with it or tease it ❑ *They that dally nicely with words may quickly make them wanton* (*Twelfth Night* 3.1)

**damask** COLOUR damask is a light-red or pink colour ❑ *'Twas just the difference/ Betwixt the constant red and mingled damask* (*As You Like It* 3.5)

**dare** 1 VERB dare means to challeng or, confront ❑ *He goes before me, and still dares me on* (*A Midsummer Night's Dream* 3.3) 2 VERB dare in this context means to present, deliver or inflict ❑ *all that fortune, death, and danger dare* (*Hamlet* 4.4)

**darkly** ADV darkly was used in this context to mean secretly or cunningly ❑ *I will go darkly to work with her* (*Measure for Measure* 5.1)

**daw** NOUN a daw was a slang term for idiot or fool (after the bird jackdaw which was famous for its stupidity) ❑ *Yea, just so much as you may take upon a knife's point and choke a daw withal* (*Much Ado About Nothing* 3.1)

**debile** ADJ debile meant weak or feeble ❑ *And debile minister great power* (*All's Well That Ends Well* 2.3)

**deboshed** ADJ deboshed was another way of saying corrupted or debauched ❑ *Men so disordered, deboshed and bold* (*King Lear* 1.4)

**decoct** VERB to decoct was to heat up, warm something ❑ *Can sodden water,/ A drench for sur-reined jades*

*... Decoct their cold blood to such valiant heat?* (*Henry V* 3.5)

**deep-revolving** ADJ deep-revolving here uses the idea that you turn something over in your mind when you are thinking hard about it and so means deep-thinking, meditating ❑ *The deep-revolving Buckingham/ No more shall be the neighbour to my counsels* (*Richard III* 4.2)

**defect** NOUN defect here means shortcoming or something that is not right ❑ *Being unprepared/ Our will became the servant to defect* (*Macbeth* 2.1)

**degree** 1 NOUN degree here means rank, standing or station ❑ *Should a like language use to all degrees,/ And mannerly distinguishment leave out/ Betwixt the prince and beggar* (*The Winter's Tale* 2.1) 2 NOUN in this context, degree means extent or measure ❑ *her offence/ Must be of such unnatural degree* (*King Lear* 1.1)

**deify** VERB if you deify something or someone you worship it or them as a God ❑ *all.. deifying the name of Rosalind* (*As You Like It* 3.2)

**delated** ADJ delated here means detailed ❑ *the scope/ Of these delated articles* (*Hamlet* 1.2)

**delicate** ADJ if something was described as delicate it meant it was of fine quality or valuable ❑ *thou wast a spirit too delicate* (*The Tempest* 1.2)

**demise** VERB in this context demise means to transmit, give or convey ❑ *what state ... Canst thou demise to any child of mine?* (*Richard III* 4.4)

**deplore** VERB to deplore means to express with grief or sorrow ❑ *Never more/Will I my master's tears to you deplore* (*Twelfth Night* 3.1)

**depose** VERB if you depose someone you make them take an oath, or swear something to be true ❑ *Depose him in the justice of his cause* (*Richard II* 1.3)

**depositary** NOUN a depositary is a trustee ❑ *Made you ... my depositary* (*King Lear* 2.4)

**derive** 1 VERB to derive means to comes from or to descend (it usually applies to people) ❑ *No part of it is mine,/This shame derives itself from unknown loins.* (*Much Ado About Nothing* 4.1) 2 VERB if you derive something from someone you inherit it ❑ *Treason is not inherited ...Or, if we derive it from our friends/What's that to me?* (*As You Like It* 1.3)

**descry** VERB to see or catch sight of ❑ *The news is true, my lord. He is descried* (*Anthony and Cleopatra* 3.7)

**desert** 1 NOUN desert means worth or merit ❑ *That dost in vile misprason shackle up/My love and her desert* (*All's Well That Ends Well* 2.3) 2 ADJ desert is used here to mean lonely or isolated ❑ *if that love or gold/Can in this desert place buy entertainment* (*As You LIke It* 2.4)

**design** 1 VERB to design means to indicate or point out ❑ *we shall see/Justice design the victor's chivalry* (*Richard II* 1.1) 2 NOUN a design is a plan, an intention or an undertaking ❑ *hinder not the honour of his design* (*All's Well That Ends Well* 3.6)

**designment** NOUN a designment was a plan or undertaking ❑ *The desperate tempest hath so bang'd the Turks,/That their designment halts* (*Othello* 2.1)

**despite** VERB despite here means to spite or attempt to thwart a plan ❑ *Only to despite them I will endeavour anything* (*Much Ado About Nothing* 2.2)

**device** NOUN a device is a plan, plot or trick ❑ *Excellent, I smell a device* (*Twelfth Night* 2.3)

**disable** VERB to disable here means to devalue or make little of ❑ *he disabled my judgement* (*As You Like It* 5.4)

**discandy** VERB here discandy means to melt away or dissolve ❑ *The hearts ... do discandy , melt their sweets* (*Anthony and Cleopatra* 4.12)

**disciple** VERB to disciple is to teach or train ❑ *He ...was/Discipled of the bravest* (*All's Well That Ends Well* 1.2)

**discommend** VERB if you discommend something you criticize it ❑ *my dialect which you discommend so much* (*King Lear* 2.2)

**discourse** NOUN discourse means conversation, talk or chat ❑ *which part of it I'll waste/With such discourse as I not doubt shall make it/Go quick away* (*The Tempest* 5.1)

**discover** VERB discover used to mean to reveal or show ❑ *the Prince discovered to Claudio that he loved my niece* (*Much Ado About Nothing* 1.2)

**disliken** VERB disguise, make unlike ❑ *disliken/The truth of your own seeming* (*The Winter's Tale* 4.4)

**dismantle** VERB to dismantle is to remove or take away ❑ *Commit a thing so monstrous to dismantle/*

*So many folds of favour (King Lear 1.1)*

**disponge** VERB disponge means to pour out or rain down ❑ *The poisonous damp of night disponge upon me (Anthony and Cleopatra 4.9)*

**distrain** VERB to distrain something is to confiscate it ❑ *My father's goods are all distrained and sold (Richard II 2.3)*

**divers** ADJ divers is an old word for various ❑ *I will give out divers schedules of my beauty (Twelfth Night 1.5)*

**doff** VERB to doff is to get rid of or dispose ❑ *make our women fight/ To doff their dire distresses (Macbeth 4.3)*

**dog** VERB if you dog someone or something you follow them or it closely ❑ *I will rather leave to see Hector than not to dog him (Troilus and Cressida 5.1)*

**dotage** NOUN dotage here means infatuation ❑ *Her dotage now I do begin to pity (A Midsummer Night's Dream 4.1)*

**dotard** NOUN a dotard was an old fool ❑ *I speak not like a dotard nor a fool (Much Ado About Nothing 5.1)*

**dote** VERB to dote is to love, cherish, care without seeing any fault ❑ *And won her soul; and she, sweet lady, dotes,/ Devoutly dotes, dotes in idolatry (A Midsummer Night's Dream 1.1)*

**doublet** NOUN a doublet was a man's close-fitting jacket with short skirt ❑ *Lord Hamlet, with his doublet all unbraced (Hamlet 2.1)*

**dowager** NOUN a dowager is a widow ❑ *Like to a step-dame or a dowage (A Midsummer Night's Dream 1.1)*

**dowdy** NOUN a dowdy was an ugly woman ❑ *Dido was a dowdy (Romeo and Juliet 2.4)*

**dower** NOUN a dower (or dowery) is the riches or property given by the father of a bride to her husband-to-be ❑ *Thy truth then by they dower (King Lear 1.1)*

**dram** NOUN a dram is a tiny amount ❑ *Why, everything adheres together that no dram of a scruple (Twelfth Night 3.4)*

**drift** NOUN drift is a plan, scheme or intention ❑ *Shall Romeo by my letters know our drift (Romeo and Juliet 4.1)*

**dropsied** ADJ dropsied means pretentious ❑ *Where great additions swell's and virtues none/ It is a dropsied honour (All's Well That Ends Well 2.3)*

**drudge** NOUN a drudge was a slave, servant ❑ *If I be his cuckold, he's my drudge (All's Well That Ends Well 1.3)*

**dwell** VERB to dwell sometimes meant to exist, to be ❑ *I'd rather dwell in my necessity (Merchant of Venice 1.3)*

**earnest** ADJ an earnest was a pledge to pay or a payment in advance ❑ *for an earnest of a greater honour/ He bade me from him call thee Thane of Cawdor (Macbeth 1.3)*

**ecstasy** NOUN madness ❑ *This is the very ecstasy of love (Hamlet 2.1)*

**edict** NOUN law or declaration ❑ *It stands as an edict in destiny. (A Midsummer Night's Dream 1.1)*

**egall** ADJ egall is an old word meaning equal ❑ *companions/Whose souls do bear an egall yoke of love* (*Merchant of Venice 2.4*)

**eisel** NOUN eisel meant vinegar ❑ *Woo't drink up eisel?* (*Hamlet 5.1*)

**eke, eke out** VERB eke meant to add to, to increase. Eke out nowadays means to make something last as long as possible – particularly in the sense of making money last a long time ❑ *Still be kind/And eke out our performance with your mind* (*Henry V Chorus*)

**elbow, out at** PHRASE out at elbow is an old phrase meaning in poor condition – as when your jacket sleeves are worn at the elbow which shows that it is an old jacket ❑ *He cannot, sir. He's out at elbow* (*Measure for Measure 2.1*)

**element** NOUN elements were thought to be the things from which all things were made. They were: air, earth, water and fire ❑ *Does not our lives consist of the four elements?* (*Twelfth Night 2.3*)

**elf** VERB to elf was to tangle ❑ *I'll … elf all my hairs in knots* (*King Lear 2.3*)

**embassy** NOUN an embassy was a message ❑ *We'll once more hear Orsino's embassy.* (*Twelfth Night 1.5*)

**emphasis** NOUN emphasis here means a forceful expression or strong statement ❑ *What is he whose grief/Bears such an emphasis* (*Hamlet 5.1*)

**empiric** NOUN an empiric was an untrained doctor sometimes called a quack ❑ *we must not … prostitute our past-cure malady/To empirics* (*All's Well That Ends Well 2.1*)

**emulate** ADJ emulate here means envious ❑ *pricked on by a most emulate pride* (*Hamlet 1.1*)

**enchant** VERB to enchant meant to put a magic spell on ❑ *Damn'd as thou art, thou hast enchanted her,/For I'll refer me to all things of sense* (*Othello 1.2*)

**enclog** VERB to enclog was to hinder something or to provide an obstacle to it ❑ *Traitors enscarped to enclog the guiltless keel* (*Othello 1.2*)

**endure** VERB to endure was to allow or to permit ❑ *and will endure/Our setting down before't.* (*Macbeth 5.4*)

**enfranchise** VERB if you enfranchised something you set it free ❑ *Do this or this;/Take in that kingdom and enfranchise that;/Perform't, or else we damn thee.'* (*Anthony and Cleopatra 1.1*)

**engage** VERB to engage here means to pledge or to promise ❑ *This to be true I do engage my life* (*As You Like It 5.4*)

**engaol** VERB to lock up or put in prison ❑ *Within my mouth you have engaoled my tongue* (*Richard II 1.3*)

**engine** NOUN an engine was a plot, device or a machine ❑ *their promises, enticements, oaths, tokens, and all these engines, of lust, are not the things they go under* (*All's Well That Ends Well 3.5*)

**englut** VERB if you were engulfed you were swallowed up or eaten whole ❑ *For certainly thou art so near the gulf,/Thou needs must be englutted.* (*Henry V 4.3*)

**enjoined** ADJ enjoined describes people joined together for the same reason ❑ *Of enjoined penitents/*

*There's four or five* (*All's Well That Ends Well 3.5*)

**entertain** 1 VERB to entertain here means to welcome or receive ❑ *Approach, rich Ceres, her to entertain.* (*The Tempest 4.1*) 2 VERB to entertain in this context means to cherish, hold in high regard or to respect ❑ *and I quake,/ Lest thou a feverous life shouldst entertain/ And six or seven winters more respect/ Than a perpetual honour.* (*Measure for Measure 3.1*) 3 VERB to entertain means here to give something consideration ❑ *But entertain it,/ And though you think me poor, I am the man/ Will give thee all the world.* (*Anthony and Cleopatra 2.7*) 4 VERB to entertain here means to treat or handle ❑ *your highness is not entertained with that ceremonious affection as you were wont* (*King Lear 1.4*)

**envious** ADJ envious meant spiteful or vindictive ❑ *he shall appear to the envious a scholar* (*Measure for Measure 3.2*)

**ere** PREP ere was a common word for before ❑ *ere this I should ha' fatted all the region kites* (*Hamlet 2.2*)

**err** VERB to err means to go astray, to make a mistake ❑ *And as he errs, doting on Hermia's eyes* (*A Midsummer Night's Dream 1.1*)

**erst** ADV erst was a common word for once or before ❑ *that erst brought sweetly forth/ The freckled cowslip* (*Henry V 5.2*)

**eschew** VERB if you eschew something you deliberately avoid doing it ❑ *What cannot be eschewed must be embraced* (*The Merry Wives of Windsor 5.5*)

**escote** VERB to escote meant to pay for, support ❑ *How are they escoted?* (*Hamlet 2.2*)

**estimable** ADJ estimable meant appreciative ❑ *I could not with such estimable wonder over-far believe that* (*Twelfth Night 2.1*)

**extenuate** VERB extenuate means to lessen ❑ *Which by no means we may extenuate* (*A Midsummer Night's Dream 1.1*)

**fain** ADV fain was a common word meaning gladly or willingly ❑ *I would fain prove so* (*Hamlet 2.2*)

**fall** NOUN in a voice or music fall meant going higher and lower ❑ *and so die/ That strain again! it had a dying fall* (*Twelfth Night 1.1*)

**false** ADJ false was a common word for treacherous ❑ *this is counter, you false Danish dogs!* (*Hamlet 4.5*)

**fare** VERB fare means to get on or manage ❑ *I fare well* (*The Taming of the Shrew Introduction 2*)

**feign** VERB to feign was to make up, pretend or fake ❑ *It is the more like to be feigned* (*Twelfth Night 1.5*)

**fie** EXCLAM fie was an exclamation of disgust ❑ *Fie, that you'll say so!* (*Twelfth Night 1.3*)

**figure** VERB to figure was to symbolize or look like ❑ *Wings and no eyes, figure unheedy haste* (*A Midsummer Night's Dream 1.1*)

**filch** VERB if you filch something you steal it ❑ *With cunning hast thou filch'd my daughter's heart* (*A Midsummer Night's Dream 1.1*)

**flout** VERB to flout something meant to scorn it ❑ *Why will you suffer her to flout me thus?* (*A Midsummer Night's Dream 3.2*)

**fond** ADJ fond was a common word meaning foolish ❑ *Shall we their fond pageant see?* (*A Midsummer Night's Dream 3.2*)

**footing** 1 NOUN footing meant landing on shore, arrival, disembarkation ❑ *Whose footing here anticipates our thoughts/ A se'nnight's speed.* (*Othello 2.1*) 2 NOUN footing also means support ❑ *there your charity would have lacked footing* (*Winter's Tale 3.3*)

**forsooth** ADV in truth, certainly, truly
❑ *I had rather, forsooth, go before you like a man* (*The Merry Wives of Windsor 3.2*)

**forswear** VERB if you forswear you lie, swear falsely or break your word ❑ *he swore a thing to me on Monday night, which he forswore on Tuesday morning* (*Much Ado About Nothing 5.1*)

**freshes** NOUN a fresh is a fresh water stream ❑ *He shall drink nought brine, for I'll not show him/ Where the quick freshes are.* (*Tempest 3.2*)

**furlong** NOUN a furlong is a measure of distance. It is the equivalent on one eight of a mile ❑ *Now would I give a thousand furlongs of sea for an acre of barren ground* (*Tempest 1.1*)

**gaberdine** NOUN a gaberdine is a cloak ❑ *My best way is to creep under his gaberdine* (*Tempest 2.2*)

**gage** NOUN a gage was a challenge to duel or fight ❑ *There is my gage, Aumerle, in gage to thine* (*Richard II 4.1*)

**gait** NOUN your gait is your way of walking or step ❑ *I know her by her gait* (*Tempest 4.1*)

**gall** VERB to gall is to annoy or irritate ❑ *Let it not gall your patience, good Iago,/ That I extend my manners* (*Othello 2.1*)

**gambol** NOUN frolic or play ❑ *Hop in his walks, and gambol in his eyes* (*A Midsummer Night's Dream 3.1*)

**gaskins** NOUN gaskins is an old word for trousers ❑ *or, if both break, your gaskins fall.* (*Twelfth Night 1.5*)

**gentle** ADJ gentle means noble or well-born ❑ *thrice-gentle Cassio!* (*Othello 3.4*)

**glass** NOUN a glass was another word for a mirror ❑ *no woman's face remember/ Save from my glass, mine own* (*Tempest 3.1*)

**gleek** VERB to gleek means to make a joke or jibe ❑ *Nay, I can gleek upon occasion* (*A Midsummer Night's Dream 3.1*)

**gust** NOUN gust meant taste, desire or enjoyment. We still say that if you do something with gusto you do it with enjoyment or enthusiasm ❑ *the gust he hath in quarrelling* (*Twelfth Night 1.3*)

**habit** NOUN habit means clothes ❑ *You know me by my habit* (*Henry V 3.6* )

**heaviness** NOUN heaviness means sadness or grief ❑ *So sorrow's heaviness doth heavier grow/ For debt that bankrupt sleep doth sorrow owe* (*A Midsummer Night's Dream 3.2*)

**heavy** ADJ if you are heavy you are said to be sad or sorrowful ❑ *Away from light steals home my heavy son* (*Romeo and Juliet 1.1*)

**hie** VERB to hie meant to hurry ❑ *My husband hies him home* (*All Well That Ends Well 4.4*)

**hollowly** ADV if you did something hollowly you did it insincerely ❏ *If hollowly invert/What best is boded me to mischief!* (*Tempest 3.1*)

**holy-water, court** PHRASE if you court holy water you make empty promises, or make statements which sound good but have no real meaning ❏ *court holy-water in a dry house is better than this rain-water out o'door* (*King Lear 3.2*)

**howsoever** ADV howsoever was often used instead of however ❏ *But howsoever strange and admirable* (*A Midsummer Night's Dream 5.1*)

**humour** NOUN your humour was your mood, frame of mind or temperament ❏ *it fits my humour well* (*As You Like It 3.2*)

**ill** ADJ ill means bad ❏ *I must thank him only,/Let my remembrance suffer ill report* (*Antony and Cleopatra 2.2*)

**indistinct** ADJ inseparable or unable to see a difference ❏ *Even till we make the main and the aerial blue/An indistinct regard.* (*Othello 2.1*)

**indulgence** NOUN indulgence meant approval ❏ *As you from crimes would pardoned be,/Let your indulgence set me free* (*The Tempest Epilogue*)

**infirmity** NOUN infirmity was weakness or fraility ❏ *Be not disturbed with my infirmity* (*The Tempest 4.1*)

**intelligence** NOUN here intelligence means information ❏ *Pursue her; and for this intelligence/If I have thanks* (*A Midsummer Night's Dream 1.1*)

**inwards** NOUN inwards meant someone's internal organs ❏ *the thought whereof/Doth like a poisonous mineral gnaw my inwards* (*Othello 2.1*)

**issue** 1 NOUN the issue of a marriage are the children ❏ *To thine and Albany's issues,/Be this perpetual* (*King Lear 1.1*) 2 NOUN in this context issue means outcome or result ❏ *I am to pray you, not to strain my speech,/To grosser issues* (*Othello*)

**kind** NOUN kind here means situation or case ❏ *But in this kind, wanting your father's voice,/The other must be held the worthier.* (*A Midsummer Night's Dream 1.1*)

**knave** NOUN a knave was a common word for scoundrel ❏ *How absolute the knave is!* (*Hamlet 5.1*)

**league** NOUN A distance. A league was the distance a person could walk in one hour ❏ *From Athens is her house remote seven leagues* (*A Midsummer Night's Dream 1.1*)

**lief, had as** ADJ I had as lief means I should like just as much ❏ *I had as lief the town crier spoke my lines* (*Hamlet 1.2*)

**livery** NOUN livery was a costume, outfit, uniform usually worn by a servant ❏ *You can endure the livery of a nun* (*A Midsummer Night's Dream 1.1*)

**loam** NOUN loam is soil containing decayed vegetable matter and therefore good for growing crops and plants ❏ *and let him have some plaster, or some loam, or some rough-cast about him, to signify wall* (*A Midsummer Night's Dream 3.1*)

**lusty** ADJ lusty meant strong ❏ *and oared/Himself with his good arms in lusty stroke/To th' shore* (*The Tempest 2.1*)

167

**maidenhead** NOUN maidenhead means chastity or virginity ❑ *What I am, and what I would, are as secret as maidenhead* (*Twelfth Night 1.5*)

**mark** VERB mark means to note or pay attention to ❑ *Where sighs and groans,/ Are made not marked* (*Macbeth 4.3*)

**marvellous** ADJ very or extremely ❑ *here's a marvellous convenient place for our rehearsal* (*A Midsummer Night's Dream 3.1*)

**meet** ADJ right or proper ❑ *tis most meet you should* (*Macbeth 5.1*)

**merely** ADV completely or entirely ❑ *Love is merely a madness* (*As You Like It 3.2*)

**misgraffed** ADJ misgraffed is an old word for mismatched or unequal ❑ *Or else misgraffed in respect of years* (*A Midsummer Night's Dream 1.1*)

**misprision** NOUN a misprision meant an error or mistake ❑ *Misprision in the highest degree!* (*Twelfth Night 1.5*)

**mollification** NOUN mollification is appeasement or a way of preventing someone getting angry ❑ *I am to hull here a little longer. Some mollification for your giant* (*Twelfth Night 1.5*)

**mouth, cold in the** PHRASE a well-known saying of the time which meant to be dead ❑ *What, must our mouths be cold?* (*The Tempest 1.1*)

**murmur** NOUN murmur was another word for rumour or hearsay ❑ *and then 'twas fresh in murmur* (*Twelfth Night 1.2*)

**murrain** NOUN murrain was another word for plague, pestilence ❑ *A murrain on your monster, and the devil take your fingers!* (*The Tempest 3.2*)

**neaf** NOUN neaf meant fist ❑ *Give me your neaf, Monsieur Mustardseed* (*A Midsummer Night's Dream 4.1*)

**nice** 1 ADJ nice had a number of meanings here it means fussy or particular ❑ *An therefore, goaded with most sharp occasions,/ Which lay nice manners by, I put you to/ The use of your own virtues* (*All's Well That Ends Well 5.1*) 2 ADJ nice here means critical or delicate ❑ *We're good... To set so rich a man/ On the nice hazard of one doubtful hour?* (*Henry IV part 1*) 3 ADJ nice in this context means carefully accurate, fastidious ❑ *O relation/ Too nice and yet too true!* (*Macbeth 4.3*) 4 ADJ trivial, unimportant ❑ *Romeo .. Bid him bethink/ How nice the quarrel was* (*Romeo and Juliet 3.1*)

**nonpareil** NOUN if you are nonpareil you are without equal, peerless ❑ *though you were crown'd/ The nonpareil of beauty!* (*Twelfth Night 1.5*)

**office** NOUN office here means business or work ❑ *Speak your office* (*Twelfth Night 1.5*)

**outsport** VERB outsport meant to overdo ❑ *Let's teach ourselves that honorable stop,/ Not to outsport discretion.* (*Othello 2.2*)

**owe** VERB owe meant own, possess ❑ *Lend less than thou owest* (*King Lear 1.4*)

**paragon** 1 VERB to paragon was to surpass or excede ❑ *he hath achieved a maid/ That paragons description and wild fame* (*Othello 2.1*) 2 VERB to paragon could also mean to compare with ❑ *I will give thee* *bloody teeth If thou with Caesar paragon again/ My man of men (Anthony and Cleopatra 1.5)*

**pate** NOUN pate is another word for head ❑ *Back, slave, or I will break thy pate across (The Comedy of Errors 2.1)*

**paunch** VERB to paunch someone is to stab (usually in the stomach). Paunch is still a common word for a stomach ❑ *Batter his skull, or paunch him with a stake (The Tempest 3.2)*

**peevish** ADJ if you are peevish you are irritable or easily angered ❑ *Run after that same peevish messenger (Twelfth Night 1.5)*

**peradventure** ADV perhaps or maybe ❑ *Peradventure this is not Fortune's work (As You Like It 1.2)*

**perforce** 1 ADV by force or violently ❑ *my rights and royalties,/ Plucked from my arms perforce (Richard II 2.3)* 2 ADV necessarily ❑ *The hearts of men, they must perforce have melted (Richard II 5.2)*

**personage** NOUN personage meant your appearance ❑ *Of what personage and years is he? (Twelfth Night 1.5)*

**pestilence** NOUN pestilence was a common word for plague or disease ❑ *Methought she purg'd the air of pestilence! (Twelfth Night 1.1)*

**physic** NOUN physic was medicine or a treatment ❑ *'tis a physic/ That's bitter to sweet end (Measure for Measure 4.6)*

**place** NOUN place means a person's position or rank ❑ *Sons, kinsmen, thanes,/ And you whose places are the nearest (Macbeth 1.4)*

**post** NOUN here a post means a messenger ❑ *there are twenty weak and wearied posts/ Come from the north (Henry IV part II 2.4)*

**pox** NOUN pox was a word for any disease during which the victim had blisters on the skin. It was also a curse, a swear word ❑ *The pox of such antic, lisping, affecting phantasims (Romeo and Juliet 2.4)*

**prate** VERB to prate means to chatter ❑ *if thou prate of mountains (Hamlet 5.1)*

**prattle** VERB to prattle is to chatter or talk without purpose ❑ *I prattle out of fashion, and I dote In mine own comforts (Othello 2.1)*

**precept** NOUN a precept was an order or command ❑ *and my father's precepts I therein do forget. (The Tempest 3.1)*

**present** ADJ present here means immediate ❑ *We'll put the matter to the present push (Hamlet 5.1)*

**prithee** EXCLAM prithee is the equivalent of please or may I ask – a polite request ❑ *I prithee, and I'll pay thee bounteously (Twelfth Night 1.2)*

**prodigal** NOUN a prodigal is someone who wastes or squanders money ❑ *he's a very fool, and a prodigal (Twelfth Night 1.3)*

**purpose** NOUN purpose is used here to mean intention ❑ *understand my purposes aright (King Lear 1.4)*

**quaff** VERB quaff was a common word which meant to drink heavily or take a big drink ❑ *That quaffing and drinking will undo you (Twelfth Night 1.3)*

**quaint** 1 ADJ clever, ingenious ❏ *with a quaint device* (*The Tempest 3.3*) 2 ADJ cunning ❏ *I'll... tell quaint lies* (*Merchant of Venice 3.4*) 3 ADJ pretty, attractive ❏ *The clamorous owl, that nightly hoots and wonders/At our quaint spirit* (*A Midsummer Night's Dream 2.2*)

**quoth** VERB an old word which means say ❏ *'Tis dinner time.' quoth I* (*The Comedy of Errors 2.1*)

**rack** NOUN a rack described clouds or a cloud formation ❏ *And, like this insubstantial pageant faded,/ Leave not a rack behind* (*The Tempest 4.1*)

**rail** VERB to rant or swear at. It is still used occasionally today ❏ *Why do I rail on thee* (*Richard II 5.5*)

**rate** NOUN rate meant estimate, opinion ❏ *My son is lost, and, in my rate, she too* (*The Tempest 2.1*)

**recreant** NOUN recreant is an old word which means coward ❏ *Come, recreant, come, thou child* (*A Midsummer Night's Dream 3.2*)

**remembrance** NOUN remembrance is used here to mean memory or recollection ❏ *our remembrances of days foregone* (*All's Well That Ends Well 1.3*)

**resolute** ADJ firm or not going to change your mind ❏ *You are resolute, then?* (*Twelfth Night 1.5*)

**revels** NOUN revels means celebrations or a party ❏ *Our revels now are ended* (*The Tempest 4.1*)

**rough-cast** NOUN a mixture of lime and gravel (sometimes shells too) for use on an outer wall ❏ *and let him have some plaster, or some loam, or some rough-cast about him, to signify wall* (*A Midsummer Night's Dream 3.1*)

**sack** NOUN sack was another word for wine ❏ *My man-monster hath drowned his tongue in sack.* (*The Tempest 3.2*)

**sad** ADJ in this context sad means serious, grave ❏ *comes me the Prince and Claudio... in sad conference* (*Much Ado About Nothing 1.3*)

**sampler** NOUN a piece of embroidery, which often showed the family tree ❏ *Both on one sampler, sitting on one cushion* (*A Midsummer Night's Dream 3.2*)

**saucy** ADJ saucy means rude ❏ *I heard you were saucy at my gates* (*Twelfth Night 1.5*)

**schooling** NOUN schooling means advice ❏ *I have some private schooling for you both.* (*A Midsummer Night's Dream 1.1*)

**seething** ADJ seething in this case means boiling – we now use seething when we are very angry ❏ *Lovers and madmen have such seething brains* (*A Midsummer Night's Dream 5.1*)

**semblative** ADJ semblative means resembling or looking like ❏ *And all is semblative a woman's part.* (*Twelfth Night 1.4*)

**several** ADJ several here means separate or different ❏ *twenty several messengers* (*Anthony and Cleopatra 1.5*)

**shrew** NOUN An annoying person or someone who makes you cross ❏ *Bless you, fair shrew.* (*Twelfth Night 1.3*)

**shroud** VERB to shroud is to hide or shelter ❏ *I will here, shroud till the dregs of the storm be past* (*The Tempest 2.2*)

**sickleman** NOUN a sickleman was someone who used a sickle to harvest crops ❏ *You sunburnt sicklemen, of August weary* (*The Tempest 4.1*)

**soft** ADV soft here means wait a moment or stop ❏ *But, soft, what nymphs are these* (*A Midsummer Night's Dream 4.1*)

**something** ADV something here means somewhat or rather ❏ *Be something scanter of your maiden presence* (*Hamlet 1.3*)

**sooth** NOUN truly ❏ *Yes, sooth; and so do you* (*A Midsummer Night's Dream 3.2*)

**spleen** NOUN spleen means fury or anger ❏ *That, in a spleen, unfolds both heaven and earth* (*A Midsummer Night's Dream 1.1*)

**sport** NOUN sport means recreation or entertainment ❏ *I see our wars/ Will turn unto a peaceful comic sport* (*Henry VI part I 2.2*)

**strain** NOUN a strain is a tune or a musical phrase ❏ *and so die/ That strain again! it had a dying fall* (*Twelfth Night 1.1*)

**suffer** VERB in this context suffer means perish or die ❏ *but an islander that hath lately suffered by a thunderbolt.* (*The Tempest 2.2*)

**suit** NOUN a suit is a petition, request or proposal (marriage) ❏ *Because she will admit no kind of suit* (*Twelfth Night 1.2*)

**sup** VERB to sup is to have supper ❏ *Go know of Cassio where he supped tonight* (*Othello 5.1*)

**surfeit** NOUN a surfeit is an amount which is too large ❏ *If music be the food of love, play on;/ Give me excess of it, that, surfeiting,/ The appetite may sicken* (*Twelfth Night 1.1*)

**swain** NOUN a swain is a suitor or person who wants to marry ❏ *take this transformed scalp/ From off the head of this Athenian swain* (*A Midsummer Night's Dream 4.1*)

**thereto** ADV thereto meant also ❏ *If she be black, and thereto have a wit* (*Othello 2.1*)

**throstle** NOUN a throstle was a name for a song-bird ❏ *The throstle with his note so true* (*A Midsummer Night's Dream 3.1*)

**tidings** NOUN tidings meant news ❏ *that upon certain tidings now arrived, importing the mere perdition of the Turkish fleet* (*Othello 2.2*)

**transgress** VERB if you transgress you break a moral law or rule of behaviour ❏ *Virtue that transgresses is but patched with sin* (*Twelfth Night 1.5*)

**troth, by my** PHRASE this phrase means I swear or in truth or on my word ❏ *By my troth, Sir Toby, you must come in earlier o' nights* (*Twelfth Night 1.3*)

**trumpery** NOUN trumpery means things that look expensive but are worth nothing (often clothing) ❏ *The trumpery in my house, go bring it hither/ For stale catch these thieves* (*The Tempest 4.1*)

**twink** NOUN In the wink of an eye or no time at all ❏ *Ay, with a twink* (*The Tempest 4.1*)

**undone** ADJ if something or someone is undone they are ruined, destroyed, brought down ❑ *You have undone a man of fourscore three* (*The Winter's Tale 4.4*)

**varlets** NOUN varlets were villains or ruffians ❑ *Say again: where didst thou leave these varlets?* (*The Tempest 4.1*)

**vaward** NOUN the vaward is an old word for the vanguard, front part or earliest ❑ *And since we have the vaward of the day* (*A Midsummer Night's Dream 4.1*)

**visage** NOUN face ❑ *when Phoebe doth behold/ Her silver visage in the watery glass* (*A Midsummer Night's Dream 1.1*)

**voice** NOUN voice means vote ❑ *He has our voices* (*Coriolanus 2.3*)

**waggish** ADJ waggish means playful ❑ *As waggish boys in game themselves forswear* (*A Midsummer Night's Dream 1.1*)

**wane** VERB to wane is to vanish, go down or get slighter. It is most often used to describe a phase of the moon ❑ *but, O, methinks, how slow/ This old moon wanes* (*A Midsummer Night's Dream 1.1*)

**want** VERB to want means to lack or to be without ❑ *a beast that wants discourse of reason/ Would have mourned longer* (*Hamlet 1.2*)

**warrant** VERB to assure, promise, guarantee ❑ *I warrant your grace* (*As You Like It 1.2*)

**welkin** NOUN welkin is an old word for the sky or the heavens ❑ *The starry welkin cover thou anon/ With drooping fog as black as Acheron* (*A Midsummer Night's Dream 3.2*)

**wench** NOUN wench is an old word for a girl ❑ *Well demanded, wench* (*The Tempest 1.2*)

**whence** ADV from where ❑ *Whence came you, sir?* (*Twelfth Night 1.5*)

**wherefore** ADV why ❑ *Wherefore, sweetheart? what's your metaphor?* (*Twelfth Night 1.3*)

**wide-chopped** ADJ if you were wide-chopped you were big-mouthed ❑ *This wide-chopped rascal* (*The Tempest 1.1*)

**wight** NOUN wight is an old word for person or human being ❑ *She was a wight, if ever such wight were* (*Othello 2.1*)

**wit** NOUN wit means intelligence or wisdom ❑ *thou didst conclude hairy men plain dealers, without wit* (*The Comedy of Errors 2.2*)

**wits** NOUN wits mean mental sharpness ❑ *we that have good wits have much to answer for* (*As You Like It 4.1*)

**wont** ADJ to wont is to be in the habit of doing something regularly ❑ *When were you wont to use my sister thus?* (*The Comedy of Errors 2.2*)

**wooer** NOUN a wooer is a suitor, someone who is hoping to marry ❑ *and of a foolish knight that you brought in one night here to be her wooer* (*Twelfth Night 1.3*)

**wot** VERB wot is an old word which means know or learn ❑ *for well I wot/ Thou runnest before me* (*A Midsummer Night's Dream 3.2*)